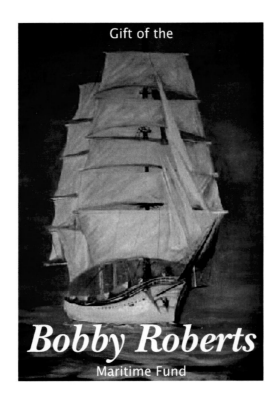

Gift of the

Bobby Roberts

Maritime Fund

The Sea Eagle

The American Crisis Series
Books on the Civil War Era

Steven E. Woodworth,
Professor of History, Texas Christian University

SERIES EDITOR

1. James L. Abrahamson. *The Men of Secession and Civil War, 1859–1861.*
2. Robert G. Tanner. *Retreat to Victory? Confederate Strategy Reconsidered.*
3. Stephen Davis. *Atlanta Will Fall: Sherman, Joe Johnston, and the Yankee Heavy Battalions.*
4. Paul Ashdown and Edward Caudill. *The Mosby Myth: A Confederate Hero in Life and Legend.*
5. Spencer C. Tucker. *A Short History of the Civil War at Sea.*
6. Richard Bruce Winders. *Crisis in the Southwest: The United States, Mexico, and the Struggle over Texas.*
7. Ethan S. Rafuse. *A Single Grand Victory: The First Campaign and Battle of Manassas.*
8. John G. Selby. *Virginians at War: The Civil War Experiences of Seven Young Confederates.*
9. Edward K. Spann. *Gotham at War: New York City, 1860–1865.*
10. Anne J. Bailey. *War and Ruin: William T. Sherman and the Savannah Campaign.*
11. Gary Dillard Joiner. *One Damn Blunder from Beginning to End: The Red River Campaign of 1864.*
12. Steven E. Woodworth. *Beneath a Northern Sky: A Short History of the Gettysburg Campaign.*
13. John C. Waugh. *On the Brink of Civil War: The Compromise of 1850 and How It Changed the Course of American History.*
14. Eric H. Walther. *The Shattering of the Union: America in the 1850s.*
15. Mark Thornton and Robert B. Ekelund Jr. *Tariffs, Blockades, and Inflation: The Economics of the Civil War.*
16. Paul Ashdown and Edward Caudill. *The Myth of Nathan Bedford Forrest.*
17. Michael B. Ballard. *U. S. Grant: The Making of a General, 1861–1863.*
18. Donald T. Collins. *The Death and Resurrection of Jefferson Davis.*
19. David Coffey. *Sheridan's Lieutenants: Phil Sheridan, His Generals, and the Final Year of the Civil War.*
20. Christopher Waldrep. *Vicksburg's Long Shadow: The Civil War Legacy of Race and Remembrance.*
21. J. Michael Martinez. *Carpetbaggers, Cavalry, and the Ku Klux Klan: Exposing the Invisible Empire During Reconstruction.*
22. Steven E. Woodworth. *Beneath a Northern Sky: A Short History of the Gettysburg Campaign, 2nd Edition.*
23. Edward Caudill and Paul Ashdown. *Sherman's March in Myth and Memory.*
24. Ethan S. Rafuse. *Robert E. Lee and the Fall of the Confederacy, 1863–1865.*
25. Alden R. Carter. *The Sea Eagle: The Civil War Memoir of Lt. Cdr. William B. Cushing.*

The Sea Eagle

The Civil War Memoir of
Lt. Cdr. William B. Cushing

Alden R. Carter

ROWMAN & LITTLEFIELD PUBLISHERS, INC.
Lanham • Boulder • New York • Toronto • Plymouth, UK

ROWMAN & LITTLEFIELD PUBLISHERS, INC.

Published in the United States of America
by Rowman & Littlefield Publishers, Inc.
A wholly owned subsidiary of The Rowman & Littlefield Publishing Group, Inc.
4501 Forbes Boulevard, Suite 200, Lanham, Maryland 20706
www.rowmanlittlefield.com

Estover Road
Plymouth PL6 7PY
United Kingdom

British Library Cataloguing in Publication Information Available

Library of Congress Cataloging-in-Publication Data:

Cushing, William Barker, 1842–1874.
 The sea eagle : the Civil War memoir of Lt. Cdr. William B. Cushing / edited by Alden
R. Carter.
  p. cm.
Includes bibliographical references and index.
 ISBN 978-0-7425-7053-5 (cloth : alk. paper) — ISBN 978-0-7425-9996-3 (electronic)
1. Cushing, William Barker, 1842–1874. 2. United States—History—Civil War,
1861–1865—Personal narratives. 3. United States—History—Civil War, 1861–1865—
Naval operations. 4. United States—History—Civil War, 1861–1865—Commando
operations. 5. Albemarle (Confederate ironclad). 6. Ship captains—United States—
Biography. 7. United States. Navy—Officers—Biography. I. Carter, Alden R. II. Title.
E467.1.C98A3 2009
973.7'8092—dc22
[B]   2009009371

Printed in the United States of America

∞ ™ The paper used in this publication meets the minimum requirements of
American National Standard for Information Sciences—Permanence of Paper
for Printed Library Materials, ANSI/NISO Z39.48-1992.

For my cousin Charles Paradise,
a lover of bees, history, and Macintosh computers.

Contents

Acknowledgments

Many thanks to all who helped with *The Sea Eagle*, particularly my editor, Niels Aaboe, and his assistant, Michelle Cassidy; my friends Judy Davis and Leigh Ashbrenner; and, as always, my wife, Carol, and my children, Brian and Siri. I am indebted to all the historians of the Civil War at sea, particularly Chris Fonvielle, author of the superb book *The Wilmington Campaign: Last Rays of Departing Home*.

ॐ

Editor's Note

William B. Cushing wrote his memoir of his Civil War service while sailing the Pacific as executive officer of the USS *Lancaster* in 1866–1867 or, more probably, while again in the Pacific as captain of the USS *Maumee* in late 1867 or early 1868. The manuscript is preserved in the National Archives as part of Record Group 45 in the Office of Naval Records Collection. Sixty-eight ledger-sized pages survive. The bottom third of the last page is missing. It appears that Cushing had nearly completed his memoir at that point, and probably no more than the bottom of that page and perhaps a page or two more are missing.

Cushing was an educated man and wrote well, with only the occasional misspelled word. In the interest of readability, I have corrected a handful of distracting errors. The rest I have left. He spelled a number of terms as two words that would today be spelled as one (e.g., *iron clad*, *head quarters*), sometimes adding a hyphen. I have retained his spellings. Cushing tended to omit hyphens in compound numbers. I have inserted the hyphens as per modern usage. In a few places, I have corrected his spelling of proper names.

His punctuation was more erratic than his spelling. I have left it largely untouched, inserting only an occasional comma and substituting lowercase letters for uppercase when he mentions compass directions. The exception to this practice is the handling of quotation marks. In the written manuscript, Cushing sometimes enclosed ship names, personal names, and place names in quotation marks. I have deleted the quotation marks and followed the modern practice of putting ship names in italics.

Cushing occasionally underlined a word or phrase for emphasis. I have followed the usual practice of rendering these in italics.

To keep footnotes to the minimum, I have identified the ships Cushing mentions in appendix 1, officers in appendix 2.

I have divided the memoir into sections for ease of reading.

I have presented the sections of *Battles and Leaders of the Civil War* as originally published in four volumes by Century Co. between 1884 and 1888, except for footnotes, which I have numbered consecutively rather than following the complicated system of typographical symbols in the original. All footnotes are by the editors of the series, by the author of the article, or by one of the editors of the *Century* magazine series on which the volumes were based.

🖎

A Note on Sources

The first full-length biography of Cushing was *Commander William Barker Cushing of the United States Navy* by Mary Hatch Edwards (New York: F. Tennyson Neely, 1898). In the following sixty years, Cushing was the subject of a number of sketches, mostly based on Edwards's work.

The most famous book on Cushing is *Lincoln's Commando* by Ralph J. Roske and Charles Van Doren (New York: Harper & Brothers, 1957). The book became a best seller thanks to the fame gained by Van Doren, a Columbia professor, during his long winning streak on the NBC quiz show *Twenty-One* in 1957–1958. His subsequent disgrace over the fixing of the show sullied both his reputation and that of the book. However, it remains a readable work, if somewhat compromised as a source by a lack of footnotes and bibliography.

The Brassey's Military Profiles series includes *Cushing: Civil War Seal* by Robert J. Schneller, Jr. (Dulles, VA: Brassey's Inc., 2004). Concise and well illustrated, it makes an excellent starting point for studying Cushing's life.

A truly first-rate scholarly biography of Cushing has yet to be published. Chris Fonvielle, a noted author on the Civil War in North Carolina, is writing a biography that may well fill that void.

Appendix 1, Ships Named in the Text, is drawn from various sources. *The Dictionary of American Fighting Ships* (DANFS), published in eight volumes by the Office of the Chief of Naval Operations, Naval History Office, between 1959 and 1981, is an excellent starting point for researching individual ships, but it is not all-inclusive or without errors.

Appendix 2, Officers Named in the Text, is also drawn from various sources. The standard sources for information on generals are the twin volumes *Generals in Gray* and *Generals in Blue*, written by Ezra J. Warner and published by Louisiana State University Press in 1959 and 1964, respectively. Warner tended to be charitable to the generals on both sides of the conflict and some further examination is often called for. Unfortunately no equivalent source exists for senior naval officers or their juniors, requiring the researcher to investigate a variety of sources. Although old and far from entirely accurate, *A Naval Encyclopedia*, published by L. R. Hamersly & Co. in 1880, contains valuable information on many of the lesser known figures.

INTRODUCTION

Before the War

William Barker Cushing packed an extraordinary amount of activity, danger, and heroism into his short life. He began his Civil War career as a disgraced midshipman and finished it as a national hero and the youngest lieutenant commander in the history of the United States Navy. Among the Union naval officers of the war, only Admiral David Farragut and, perhaps, Admiral David Dixon Porter stood as high in the public esteem.

Romantics can find hints aplenty of Cushing's bravery and thirst for fame among the distant progenitors of the Cushing clan as identified by Warren Cushing of the University of California at Irvine. The earliest common ancestor was the Viking warrior Hrolf Nefja, born about AD 826. A follower of Harald Fairhair, he was named earl of Throndjem and Maeras following Harald's unification of Norway in 872. Among Hrolf's grandsons and great-grandsons were some of the most famous warriors of the Viking Age. Eric Thorvaldsen, commonly known as Eric the Red, discovered Greenland in 982, subsequently colonizing what was then a temperate seacoast. His son, Leif Erikson, reached Newfoundland about 1000. Another of Hrolf's grandsons Gongu Hrolf, known to history as Rollo, led the Viking conquest of Normandy. Rollo's illegitimate son William invaded England in 1066, trading in his nickname William the Bastard for the more attractive William the Conqueror. A third of Hrolf's grandsons was Cu, who invaded southwestern Ireland. His descendants, through his son Cuson, continued to hold sway in Cork, Tipperary, and Limerick until the time of Cromwell. Eventually the name Cuson became Cushing.

Lieutenant William Barker Cushing in 1864.
The original photograph is in the collections of the U.S. National Archives. Naval History
and Heritage Command.

Had Will Cushing known of his famous ancestors—and that is doubtful at best—he would probably have found their history attractive. For all the grimness of the Civil War, it was in the beginning a romantic enterprise for many who rushed to defend the banners of Union or Confederacy in the spring of 1861. The literate among them had wiled away many hours on city block, rural farm, army post, or patrolling ship reading the works of Sir Walter Scott, James Fenimore Cooper, Alexandre Dumas, and the other popular romantic novelists of the first half of the nineteenth century. The hard lessons of war would disabuse most of the young soldiers and sailors of their romantic preconceptions. Yet for some, and Will Cushing seems to have been among them, the war remained a high adventure from beginning to end.

The first of Will Cushing's direct ancestors to immigrate to America was Matthew Cushing (1588–1660). Born in Hingham, Norfolk, he sailed aboard the *Diligent* from Gravesend for Massachusetts with his wife and five children in 1638. He was already fifty years old, and his reasons for leaving England were apparently religious rather than economic. Most of the passengers aboard were members of the Anglican parish in Hingham and supporters of their puritan rector in an ecclesiastical dispute with his high-church bishop. From Boston, the party traveled to Hingham, Massachusetts, founded a few years before by neighbors from home. (In 1637, a young weaver's apprentice, Samuel Lincoln, had also settled in Hingham, where he would marry and become Abraham Lincoln's great-great-grandfather.) Matthew Cushing set up a shop, farmed, and took a modest part in public affairs. Whatever inclination Matthew's descendents had to take to the sea or to seek fame, fortune, or anything else on far fields and seas was apparently well suppressed for the next several generations. In the main they were farmers and tradesmen, living within ten or twenty miles of the ancestral home in Hingham, which would remain in the family until 1887.

Will's paternal grandfather, Zattu, born in Plymouth, Massachusetts, in 1770, revealed a more adventuresome bent. The Cushing family sided with the Revolutionary cause, and Zattu celebrated the American victory at Saratoga in the autumn of 1777 by slipping out of his school in Plymouth after dark and "walking, running, and leaping with joy" as he carried the news to the family farm ten miles away.

Zattu was apprenticed to a shipbuilder in his teens. At twenty-one, he left Massachusetts for the frontier of upstate New York. He married Rachel Buckingham in Ballston Spa north of Albany in 1795. The young couple settled in Paris, south of Troy, New York. He apparently took up the shipbuilding trade again, superintending the construction of the vessel *Good Hope* on an island near Erie, Pennsylvania, in 1799. In the winter of 1805, Zattu and Rachel loaded their five children and household possessions aboard a sledge, trekking through the snowy woods and across the lake ice to Fredonia, New York. Among the children was five-year-old Milton Buckingham Cushing, who would become William B. Cushing's father. Zattu prospered in Fredonia, engaging in business and becoming a justice of the Niagara County Court. Retiring from the court in 1825, he organized a company and built the canal boat *Fredonia Enterprise* to ply the recently completed Erie Canal. The venture was a success, and the family became modestly wealthy. Zattu's prosperity enabled him to send Milton to Hamilton Literary and Theological Institute (today's Colgate) for a degree in medicine.

Milton Cushing established his medical practice in Zanesville, Ohio, where he married Abigail Tupper in 1823. They had four children together before her death in 1833. The younger of Will's half sisters, Abigail, died in infancy. The remaining half sister, Rowena (b. 1829), and his half brothers

Benjamin (b. 1825) and Edward (b. 1827) were still part of the Cushing household at the time of Will's birth in 1842. Dr. Cushing married Mary Baker Smith in 1836. Their first child, Milton, was born in 1837, the year the family moved to Milwaukee, Wisconsin, then a town of about eight hundred. Another son, Howard, was born in 1838 and a third, Walter (who did not survive infancy), in 1839. Mrs. Cushing disliked Milwaukee, and that year the family moved to a log cabin twenty-five miles west of Milwaukee and a few miles north of Waukesha (then known as Prairieville) where a village was springing up on the shores of Lake Nagawicka. The coming of a doctor was very welcome, and the Cushings' new neighbors elected him justice of the peace and chairman of the board of supervisors of the township of Nemahbin. In 1848, years after the Cushings had departed, the village was renamed Delafield, the name by which it is known today.

Dr. and Mrs. Cushing added another son to the family in January 1841 with the birth of Alonzo, who would become Will's constant childhood companion. Will was born on November 4, 1842, the last of the Cushing boys. Two sisters would follow. Mary Rachel was born in 1845 but lived less than a year. Mary Isabel was born in 1847. By then the family had moved on to Chicago, where Dr. Cushing set up his practice near the waterfront.

Nearly all the biographies of Will's early years recount a tale told by his sister Mary Isabel many years after his death. At age three, Will donned his father's top hat and set off to explore. Seeing a boat leaving from one of the nearby wharves, Will scurried to get aboard. Whether he was late, clumsy, or too stubborn to accept defeat, Will's pursuit took him over the end of the wharf. A sailor on the dock jumped in and rescued him. Queried about his name, Will answered, "Will Coon," the family's nickname for him. Unable to get more from the soaking child, the sailor took him home to his wife and then set about making inquiries. Meanwhile, the Cushing home was in a frenzy, the blame for Will's disappearance settling on his half sister Rowena, who had let him escape her care. Twenty-four hours later, Rowena salvaged some self-respect when she discovered Will at the sailor's house, his ambitions of world travel abandoned for the moment but otherwise not unhappy with his adventure.

The family's perambulations were about to resume in any event, though the cause would be unwelcome. Dr. Cushing's frail health was failing, and in the fall of 1846 he decided to investigate a move south. He spent the winter with a cousin in Vicksburg, Mississippi. Feeling somewhat restored, he returned north in the spring, stopping in Columbus, Ohio, to talk to an acquaintance, the rising lawyer and antislavery orator Salmon P. Chase. Dr. Cushing, also a passionate abolitionist, convinced Chase to take his son, Benjamin, into his law office. Getting his eldest son situated was Dr. Cushing's final accomplishment. On his way to rejoin his family in Chicago, he sickened, dying in a hotel room in Gallipolis, Ohio, on April 22, 1847, at the age of forty-six. His widow came to take his body home to Fredonia for burial in the family plot.

At five, Will was old enough to grieve for the good man who had been his father. The loss of his father and the specter of an uncertain longevity may well have inculcated a certain fatalism in Will from an early age. His reckless disregard for personal safety and his thirst for military glory were, if we accept this theory, a compensation for what he expected to be—and indeed proved to be—a short life. Dr. Cushing's children were a short-lived brood even by the standards of the nineteenth century. Both of Will's half brothers and his remaining half sister would die well before he began his Civil War service: Benjamin in 1850, Edward in 1852, and Rowena in 1858. In all, Dr. Cushing sired eleven children, outliving his first wife and three of his children. Only Milton, his eldest by his second wife, Mary, would live to a greater age than Dr. Cushing, dying at fifty. The redoubtable Mary Cushing would outlive all of them except her daughter Mary Isabel, who would die at the age of forty-five in 1892, a year after her mother passed away at eighty-four.

Will's half brother Benjamin went to work in Chase's office, as his father had planned. With Chase as a patron, he might have risen to great heights, but he died of tuberculosis less than three years later. Chase went on to become a prominent senator and a candidate for the Republican nomination for president in 1856 and 1860. Lincoln made him secretary of the treasury, placing on him the heavy burden of financing the fight to preserve the Union. In 1864, Lincoln appointed him chief justice of the Supreme Court, an office he would fill with great distinction.

During his time in the Lincoln administration, Chase extended his patronage to several prominent officers, including the brilliant but erratic William S. Rosecrans. It does not appear that Will sought to capitalize on his family's connection with Chase, although Chase did fondly recall Benjamin when he met Will during the war. Will would never share his father's and Chase's deep commitment to the abolitionist cause. His personal correspondence before and during the war contains some negative comments and more than a few crudely playful characterizations of African Americans, but on the whole he does not seem to have been any more racially insensitive than the majority of white Northerners of his time.

Like many soldiers and sailors, Cushing appears to have moderated his views as he had more contact with "contrabands," "the peculiar institution," and the growing number of African Americans in Northern uniform. The navy itself was partially integrated, African Americans serving as coal heavers and occasionally as deckhands. In southern waters, a few served as pilots on Union vessels. Among them was the renowned Robert Smalls, a twenty-two-year-old slave who smuggled his wife and children and several other African American families aboard the Confederate transport ship *Planter* at Charleston in the early morning hours of May 13, 1862. Donning the captain's broad-brimmed hat to disguise his silhouette, Smalls steamed the *Planter* boldly past Fort Sumter and Confederate picket vessels to surrender the ship and its cargo of munitions to an astounded Union blockading squadron. (Later, General Quincy Gilmore would dismiss the white officer who was subsequently given command of the *Planter*, appointing Smalls in his place.) Cushing would certainly have heard of the *Planter*'s escape, and no doubt would have admired Smalls's daring. Some indication of Cushing's changing attitude about race seems indicated by his avoidance of the terms "nigger" and "darky" (with a few exceptions of the latter) in favor of "negro" in his postwar memoir. Nor is there evidence that he ever treated African Americans in service or out with anything but fairness.

In the summer after her husband's death, Will's mother, Mary, moved the family from Chicago to Fredonia. Her father-in-law, Zattu, had died in 1839. His estate was divided among his numerous offspring, most of whom were raising their own families in Fredonia and its vicinity. With the small estate left by her husband, a modest collection raised by her in-laws, and some money from her father, Mrs. Cushing purchased a home and opened a school, the Fredonia Academy. The school quickly became a success, providing the income she would need to raise her children and stepchildren.

Cushing wrote nothing of his early years in his memoir, but elsewhere his recollections of his Fredonia childhood were fond. The town of three thousand, some three miles south of Lake Erie, must have seemed quiet after the bustle of booming Chicago. But Will and his slightly older brother Alonzo found plenty of adventures nevertheless. Will, the more confident and assertive of the two, became the leader of the neighborhood boys. He organized their games, led fishing, apple-stealing, and berrying expeditions, and concocted their practical jokes. For a time, he had them organized along military lines as "the Muss Company."

Will enjoyed the companionship of girls, particularly that of his cousin Mary Edwards, who became his lifelong friend and correspondent. He charmed adult women. His first teacher was so taken with Will that she called him a "hero in embryo." Even his strong and resolute mother could never quite find it in her heart to punish Will as severely as his transgressions warranted. Will's fondness for females might have opened a less pugnacious boy to derision by his male classmates, but Will was a prodigious fighter, whipping any boy who challenged his character or right to lead. His victories came not from physical superiority—like all the Cushing men he was slight—but from the suddenness of his fury and the ferocity of his attack.

Although Will does not appear to have been a great reader of the popular romantic fiction of his time, there seems something almost chivalric about his gallantry toward women, love of single combat, and the rigorous—indeed knightly—standards he used to take the measure of men and boys. Age, education, and position meant little to him if a man could not otherwise demonstrate character worthy of respect. Those lacking became fair game for derision and practical jokes. In Fredonia, a schoolmaster in the neighborhood was one of those whom Will found unworthy. Leaving his mother's academy, where he'd spent the morning confined, nine-year-old Will would arrive at the other school during noon recess, climb a fence, and summon the boys he had organized as the "Muss Company" with a loud whistle. Ignoring the schoolmaster's shouts, the boys would rush to form in ranks, and Will would march them away on an adventure. When the distraught schoolmaster objected to Mrs. Cushing, she chided the man for allowing a child to wreck the discipline of his school. Nevertheless, she forbade Will to harass the schoolmaster further and ordered him to disband the Muss Company.

He did not, however, abandon his strict standards for measuring other men and boys. The family's scholarly minister preferred to study late and sleep late. He hired Will to feed the chickens and drive in the cows, cautioning the boy not to arrive too early. Will, however, considered the minister a slugabed, a state not to be tolerated even in a man of the cloth. Not long after daylight, Will would arrive singing and clattering a stick along the fence. The minister's remonstrances had no more effect than the schoolmaster's had, and the household had to alter its schedule to fit Will's standards. Will was not rehired the following summer.

It wasn't that Will resented authority so much as he refused to accept it when wielded by those he considered lacking in manly virtue. That attitude would cost him dearly at the Naval Academy and frequently put him at odds with his seniors during the Civil War. But when Will judged a boy or a man worthy of his respect, his loyalty became absolute. He ignored his cautious brother Alonzo's protests, visiting a playmate quarantined with smallpox by climbing to his second-floor window. The visits continued for days until the boy's father marched him home and complained to Mrs. Cushing that he couldn't keep Will out. (Fortunately, none of the Cushings came down with the disease.) That loyalty would carry over into adulthood. In his early service in the Civil War, Will served under one of his former instructors, Lieutenant Charles W. Flusser, aboard the USS *Commodore Perry*. He idolized Flusser and was distraught when he heard of the older man's death in battle against the CSS *Albemarle*, vowing, "I shall never rest until I have avenged his death." That promise would lead Will to his most famous and dangerous raid.

Will's path to naval fame began when his uncle Francis Smith Edwards was elected to Congress in 1854. In the summer of 1855, Edwards visited the Cushing home to tell Will and his mother that he had procured Will a position as a congressional page for the fall of 1856. He was also trying to secure Alonzo an appointment to West Point, and there was a possibility he could manage a similar appointment for Will at one of the nation's service academies in a year or two.

Will was delighted with the prospect of escaping small-town Fredonia and its provincial attitudes for the wider world. He buckled down to his studies. Always happier in the outdoors, he was never particularly studious, but he had a quick mind and could master a subject if he saw utility in it. He was good at mathematics, appreciated history, and wrote well in a clear hand. He detested Latin but managed to absorb enough to graduate from the Fredonia Academy in the spring of 1856.

By the time Will struggled through his last lessons in Latin, tensions between North and South had risen to a new and disturbing level. The Kansas-Nebraska Act of 1854, a well-meaning compromise that had codified the concept of popular sovereignty, was proving a catastrophe for the political parties, the country, and especially Kansas, where pro- and antislavery forces were turning increasingly violent in the battle to determine if the territory would become a slave or free state. In January 1856, the prominent abolitionist preacher Henry Ward Beecher announced that the Sharps rifle had the moral force of the Bible in Kansas. In upstate New York, where abolitionist sympathies ran strong, Beecher's supporters gathered subscriptions to send Sharps rifles—"Beecher Bibles"—to antislavery Jayhawkers in Kansas. Proslavery sympathizers in the South responded with fund drives to finance proslavery settlers and gangs of border ruffians from Missouri.

Will was only thirteen and had little interest in politics, but in the spring and summer of 1856 it was almost impossible for anyone to ignore the news coming over the telegraph and filling the newspapers. In Lawrence, Kansas, on May 21, a proslavery mob led by Topeka's sheriff wrecked two newspapers and burned the Free-State Hotel. On May 22, Congressman Preston Brooks of South Carolina attacked Massachusetts senator Charles Sumner on the floor of the United States Senate, beating him so viciously that Sumner would need more than two years to recover. On May 25, the violent abolitionist

John Brown took revenge for the "sack of Lawrence" by brutally murdering five proslavery settlers with a broadsword at Pottawatomie Creek, Kansas.

That summer, Will would have read or heard of Preston Brooks's cold self-justification for his beating of Sumner, his disdainful resignation, and his reelection within weeks by constituents who saw him as a hero. A presidential campaign was underway amid the realignment of the two-party system. The Whig Party, feeble for a decade, had all but expired. The Democratic Party was split increasingly along sectional lines. Orphaned Whigs, disaffected Democrats, and one-time members of the defunct Free Soil Party joined the new Republican Party with its antislavery platform. The Republicans nominated the famous explorer John Charles Frémont. The Democrats nominated James Buchanan, a lackluster former senator from Pennsylvania whose major attraction was that he had been serving as minister to Britain for several years, studiously avoiding any involvement in the debate that was dividing the nation.

Will moved to Washington in the late summer of 1856 to begin his duties as a congressional page. He found life as a page tedious, requiring long periods of quiet sitting as debates droned on in the House of Representatives. Yet he performed his duties with enough enthusiasm to win the notice of a number of congressmen. In November Buchanan defeated Frémont for the presidency, but the Republicans won enough seats in Congress to block expansion of slavery. Will's uncle was among the defeated, but he would hold his seat until the new Congress convened in March.

For some months, Will lived with his uncle's family, but with winter coming on, the Edwards' apartment became increasingly cramped. In December, Will took quarters at Washington House, where many of the pages lived. The move took him away from daily contact with his beloved cousin Mary, but he enjoyed asserting his natural gift for leadership in organizing his fellow pages for rambles and adventures about the streets of the rough and unfinished capital.

Like the nation, Washington was still trying to define itself. The wide avenues radiated in the splendid design laid out by L'Enfant. But the streets were muddy, many of the public buildings (including the capitol) still incomplete, and the undrained swamps beyond the city noisome with the reek of raw sewage. Police and fire service were desperately inadequate, and the dark side streets with their brothels, taverns, and gambling dens provided rich opportunities for trouble. No doubt the pages found some, but there was safety in numbers and Will's fearless leadership. At any rate, the police reports and victim lists published in the papers do not include the name of a lad from western New York named William B. Cushing.

Although Will dismissed much that he heard of the debates in the House as "nonsense," he would nevertheless have heard some stirring oratory and vitriolic debate in chamber, cloakroom, and hall. Preston Brooks swaggered through the House, sporting one of the dozens of canes sent him by admirers. In "Bleeding Kansas," the factions warred over rival slave-state and free-state constitutions. In the Supreme Court, the justices deliberated the case of the slave Dred Scott, who claimed the right to petition the Court for his freedom because his owner had once taken him to a state declared free in the Missouri Compromise of 1820. On March 4, 1860, Will watched Buchanan's inauguration, impressed with the sight of the tall, dignified president if not with his windy two-hour speech.

Since Christmas, Will had become a regular visitor to the home of his mother's cousin, Commodore Joseph Smith, chief of the Bureau of Navy Yards and Docks. Then in his mid-sixties, Smith was a solidly built man with iron-gray hair and the unmistakable air of a man used to wielding authority. His son, Joseph Jr., was a navy lieutenant, and it's possible that he, too, occasionally joined their talks. Will, who didn't extend respect readily, stood in awe of the elder Smith. He plied the commodore with questions about his almost half century of service. Although we have no verbatim record of their conversations, we can easily imagine the subjects the old sailor and the eager youngster covered in their long evenings. Smith was one of the principal architects of the conversion of the fleet from sail to steam. Handling sail was still essential to the seafarer's art, since ships on patrol or in long transits required a more economical method of propulsion than coal-fired steam plants. But the advantages of steam power for maneuvering inshore or for propulsion when winds fell had been proven in commercial service in the half century since Robert Fulton's *Clermont* had first steamed from New York to Albany in a scant thirty-two hours.

The navy began building oceangoing warships with auxiliary steam engines in the early 1840s. As captains grew more comfortable with steam, it became the preferred motive power so long as coal was available. The first of the navy's steamers were side-wheelers, but John Ericsson's *Princeton*, commissioned in 1843, demonstrated the advantages of screw propulsion. The navy's last all-sail warship, the *Constellation*, was completed in 1854.[1] That same year, Congress authorized the building of six *Merrimack*-class screw-driven steam frigates, which Smith expected would be among the world's most powerful warships. But how long they could hold that distinction was becoming a worrisome question.

Parallel with the introduction of steam to warships was the development of a new class of heavy, shell-firing, naval cannon. For all the punch the new

---

[1]The *Constellation* is preserved in Baltimore harbor, where it was long considered a modernization of the original Federalist-era frigate *Constellation*, a sister of the *Constitution*. However, scholarship in recent years has proved that the 1854 ship was entirely new, although built with funds budgeted by Congress for an overhaul of the original frigate.

Merrimacks would deliver with their massive Dahlgren shell guns, their hulls would be as vulnerable as those of ships built a century before. Naval designers reacted to the new guns with plans to add armor to warships. Traditionalists resisted the idea, warning of a decrease in speed and handling, terrible iron splinters from the impact of shells, and the strain on wooden hulls already taxed with the weight of steam engines. All the traditionalists' objections had validity and would in time lead to more design changes, most importantly the adoption of iron and steel hulls in future generations of warships. But in the meantime, the need for armor would require some awkward compromises.

The effectiveness of the new shell guns was proven some three years before the evenings Smith and Will spent together. On November 30, 1853, a Russian squadron used Paixhans shell guns to annihilate a Turkish squadron at the battle on Sinope on the Black Sea coast of Turkey. The battle led to British and French entry into the Crimean War in the spring of 1854 on the side of Turkey. Though the allies enjoyed a huge advantage in ships, Russian forts and shore batteries forced the allies to bombard from long range and with little effect. The British and French began building ironclad batteries that could survive close enough to shore to deliver effective fire. In October 1855, the French floating batteries *Dévastation*, *Tonnante*, and *Lave* engaged the Russian fort at Kinburn at the mouth of the Dnieper. The batteries were cumbersome, flat-bottomed craft, but their four and a half inches of iron plate withstood the Russian fire virtually without damage, forcing the fort's surrender in less than four hours. The Crimean War ended in the spring of 1856, and the erstwhile allies returned to their own naval rivalry, which, in Will's final two years at the Naval Academy, would produce the world's first oceangoing ironclads, the French wooden-hulled frigate *La Gloire* (1860) and the all-iron British frigate *Warrior* (1861).

For all its reputation for traditionalism and shell-backed resistance to change, the United States Navy in the antebellum years was the more innovative of the services. Captain Robert F. Stockton had sponsored the *Princeton*, John Ericsson's screw-driven, iron-hulled sloop. Commodore John Dahlgren designed the navy's family of modern shell guns. Commodore Andrew Foote led the fight to end flogging and the rum ration to improve the lives of sailors. Commodore Smith continued to champion improved ship and engine design.[2] The greatest problem facing the navy was not so much a lack of vision as a parsimonious Congress. Yet the navy that Smith described to young Will Cushing was not an archaic institution but a service fully involved in the new industrial age. It was a navy in which an energetic and daring young man could rise.

---

[2] In 1861 Smith would chair the committee that approved plans for Ericsson's *Monitor*, as well as the woeful ironclad *Galena* and the powerful ironclad frigate *New Ironsides*.

We do not know if Smith mused in his evenings with Will on the possibilities of civil war and the naval strategies that would be available to a rebellious South. If he did, it seems likely that he would have predicted a strategy dependent on commerce raiders, blockade-runners, and ironclads. With its limited industrial capacity, the South could not hope to build a fleet to compete with that of the North. But it could build ships that would bedevil a navy attempting to dominate the sea-lanes and the South's long coastline. Such would become the reality in a few short years, and it would fall to Will to play a role out of all proportion to his youth in the eventual defeat of that strategy.

At some point in their conversations, they first discussed a naval career for Will. Smith cautioned the youngster—in whose character he no doubt saw more than a spark of impishness—that naval discipline had limited patience. Will promised to behave himself, and the commodore promised to investigate getting him an appointment to the Naval Academy. As Will suffered through the long hours of debate in the House that spring, Smith and Will's uncle Francis Edwards succeeded in securing an appointment. Will was overjoyed. He later wrote to his cousin Mary: "I had rather be an officer on a man-of-war than President of the United States."

Will spent the summer at home in Fredonia with his brother Alonzo, who would enter West Point in the fall. They chaffed each other on their chosen military professions, referring to each other as "tar" and "sojer." But they had their serious conversations, too, as sectional tensions increased and the word "secession" gained currency in the newspapers and on the lips of citizens north and south.

Will Cushing entered the United States Naval Academy at Annapolis, Maryland, in the fall of 1857, two months shy of his fifteenth birthday. Until his junior year, he would be the youngest midshipman at the academy. In 1857, the Naval Academy was only a dozen years old and poorly housed in the remains of the 1808 army post of Fort Severn on a point bounded by Annapolis Harbor, the Severn River, and College Creek. About 150 midshipmen in four classes lived in five decrepit barracks, the instructors—still mainly civilian—in somewhat better buildings nearby. Classes were held in the recitation hall, the largest building on the campus. An observatory, a dining hall and library, a chapel, and a store comprised the other principal buildings. Probably poor living conditions as much as academics or discipline were responsible for a graduation rate of only 22 percent in the first twelve years of the academy's existence.

Discipline was notoriously loose in the early years of the academy. Walls separated the academy grounds from the city streets of Annapolis, but they presented little barrier for midshipmen intent on spending a night on the town. They drank in the taverns, hurrahed in the streets, and stormed the statehouse in mock attacks. By the time Will arrived at the academy, the authorities had stiffened discipline, increasing the penalty for truancy and tightening the night watch with more civilian watchmen and a midshipman-hating Newfoundland dog.

For a lad of Will's temperament, the stricter the discipline, the more he enjoyed flaunting it. He led "Frenching" expeditions into town, often to Rosenthal's Tavern, where the midshipmen drank beer far into the night. Sneaking back to his barracks after one such outing, he encountered the Newfoundland and only succeeded in escaping at the cost of the seat of his trousers. But, as he wrote airily to his cousin Mary, "they were by no means my best pair."

Supposedly, liquor and tobacco were banned in the barracks, but Will and his mates indulged in both with enthusiasm during all-night bull sessions. They stole food from the mess, discharged the saluting guns in the night, and howled outside the windows of disliked professors. Practical jokes were Will's specialty, from the pail of cold water balanced atop a door to douse an inspecting officer to the potentially lethal trick of loading the morning gun with bricks and stones so that it would spray a charge of ersatz grapeshot into the river to the immense discomfort of early fishermen.

A year after Will's arrival, Captain George S. Blake, the academy's portly and aging superintendent, attempted to improve discipline by instituting an hour's drill a day under the command of Professor Lockwood, a West Point graduate. The midshipmen complained bitterly that they were not "sojers." They despised Lockwood, burning him in effigy and imitating his stutter. The much-taxed Lockwood stuttered the worse under the pressure. On a day glorious to all the midshipmen present, he marched the "middies" along the banks of the Severn only to begin stuttering on the command "halt" as they approached perilously close to the shore. Will supposedly hissed "keep going" or something of the sort from his place in the fourth rank. On the middies marched, off the bank and into the river, dragging their boat howitzers behind them into the ooze of the low-tide mud. Some were already swimming for the far shore by the time the wretched Lockwood finally overcame his stutter.

Though such moments of sublime absurdity helped to alleviate the long periods of boredom, Will was restless. Despite his promise to Commodore Smith to behave himself, he continued to test the limits of naval discipline. He might not have survived retribution into his first-class year without his glibness and practiced look of innocence. Both had done him good service in Fredonia, and he polished them considerably in the Naval Academy's debating club, the Lawrence Literary Society. But even Will could not talk or feign his way out of every difficulty, and he accumulated a dangerous number of demerits every year. A midshipman was allowed 200 before the navy would expel him or, in navy parlance, "restore the midshipman to his friends." He accumulated 99 as a fourth-class midshipman, 188 as a third-class, 157 as a second-class, and 147 by February of his first-class year, when naval discipline finally lashed back with full fury.

For all his demerits and brushes with authority, Will was determined on becoming a naval officer. As he had at his mother's academy in Fredonia, he worked diligently at the academic subjects that promised utility in his chosen profession. In his second-class year, he ranked ninth of thirty-seven academically, though his list of demerits dropped him far down in overall class ranking. More of the instructor positions were being assumed by regular navy officers, and Will was probably "cut some slack" by some of the weather-beaten lieutenants who saw in Will the makings of an officer. He loved the sea and loved the navy of tall masts, rolling waves, thudding engines, and thundering guns. He thrived on his summer cruises between his fourth- and third-class years and his second- and first-class years. During the academic year, he was vexed by terrible colds, but at sea his health improved despite the poor diet and long hours. He was nimble and fearless, scrambling to the rigging in all hours and sea conditions. He got his sea legs quickly and was untroubled by seasickness. When the *Plymouth* sailed for Europe on Will's first-class cruise, he took to the quarterdeck like he'd been born to it. He knew navigation, had a sense of the behavior of the ship beneath him, and never hesitated to issue an order.

During port calls, Will and his friends gorged themselves in restaurants, where they could at last eat decent food. They enjoyed the balls where they could dance in their dress uniforms with pretty girls. After the *Plymouth*, outbound for Europe, made a visit to Hampton Roads, Will wrote Mary sardonically about the opportunity to observe the FFVs (First Families of Virginia). Back at sea, he wrote ecstatically about his first real storm. Beneath the forgivable braggadocio of a young man on a high adventure, his letters revealed both the hardheaded Yankee pragmatism of his forebearers and the mysticism of a Jonathan Edwards watching God's power played out in the tumult of the elements.

Back at the academy for his final year in the fall of 1860, boredom reasserted itself. He had never been good at languages and despised the foppish Spanish professor, "Don" Edward Roget, who continually found him wanting in recitation. Will plotted revenge for the humiliation. He fell back on the time-honored trick of balancing a pail of water atop a partly open door.

Most instructors, particularly those who had gone to the academy them-selves, learned to test a door for the slight resistance that would reveal the gag. Not so Professor Roget. Dressed in his best courting clothes, he stepped boldly through his door on a brisk evening and received a dousing. Will was ecstatic, the professor furious. He could not prove Will's guilt, but he had plenty of reason to suspect him.

It is hard not to be a little embarrassed for both professor and pupil in their petty feud, given the national crisis building beyond the academy's walls in the wake of Lincoln's election that November. The Naval Academy never quite split into the warring camps found at West Point, but quarrels and fist-fights broke out daily. Pugnacious as Will ordinarily was, he seems to have remained mainly an observer, writing to his cousin Mary that he thought the South had been "deeply wronged." Still, he had no doubt where his loyalties lay, writing her on December 12:

> Midn. are every day resigning. Every Southerner has orders to resign as soon as their states secede. Secession speeches are made by the South Carolinians and Georgians, and there is not a Southern man but hopes and believes that the world now views for the last time this great Republic. . . . Matters can not be improved except by a miracle; and unless that miracle happens, the ship of State, which has been so long on a lee shore, must go down carrying with it the Naval Academy; which is but a speck on its deck. . . . But if it comes to blows between the North and the South, I will shed the last drop of my blood for the state of New York. If this place does break up, I will get my graduating papers. If it does not, I will get them all the same, but in one case it will be in June, and in the other it will be—Well! may be, in less than a month.

On December 17, South Carolina seceded. By February, Mississippi, Florida, Alabama, Georgia, Louisiana, and Texas had followed. The border states tottered. Secessionists in pro-Southern Baltimore vowed that Federal troops would never march through on the way to defending Washington. The Naval Academy, with its cannons and munitions, prepared to defend itself. Armed soldiers and sailors guarded the gates. Even then, Will and Professor Roget had time for their feud.

It is hard to understand why Will pushed his luck so far. Perhaps he was in such a state of excitement that he did not fully weigh the chances he was taking. In early January, he clashed with Superintendent Blake. Will had received a week's leave to nurse a sick aunt in Washington. Blake assumed that he meant Commodore Smith's wife, but when he chanced to meet Smith and inquired as to his wife's health, Smith replied that she was fine. No doubt already sick of hearing of Will's escapades, Blake called him to his office and accused him of lying. Will lost his temper and called Blake a liar. Eventually, the matter was sorted out, but the effrontery of Will's reply continued to rankle Blake.

A week or so after, Professor Roget appeared at Blake's door to give an angry account of the latest outrage perpetrated by Midshipman 1/c Cushing. The unfortunate professor had been painfully bitten by a carthorse. In the hard way of young men, Will and the other midshipmen found the misfortune hilarious. Coming into class with his shoulder heavily bandaged, Roget found a group of laughing midshipman gathered around Will's desk. He stepped into the throng and saw skillfully rendered on the flyleaf of Will's Spanish text a cartoon of Roget biting the carthorse. The caption read: "The poor Don, he bit the hoss!" Outraged, Roget seized the book, snapping that the horse had bitten him, not the other way around. The midshipmen exploded in merriment. For the rest of the period, they found any excuse to burst into laughter, eventually sending the professor storming out the door to find Blake.

Will survived this incident, too—perhaps because Blake didn't want to arouse Smith's anger by dismissing Will for a mere cartoon—but he and Roget began looking for an excuse to "restore the midshipman to his friends." That Will did not fully appreciate his precarious situation became evident when he failed his midyear Spanish examination. Blake sent a report to the Navy Department: "Deficient at February semi-annual examination, 1861. Midshipman William B. Cushing. Deficient in Spanish. Aptitude for study: good. Habits of study: irregular. General conduct: bad. Aptitude for Naval Service: not good. Not recommended for continuance at the Academy." Will was summoned to Washington, where, on March 23, 1861, Secretary of the Navy Welles informed him of Blake's recommendation and demanded his resignation.

We can only imagine how painful it was for Will to write of his disgrace to his mother and his cousin Mary. Alonzo was doing well at West Point, and that must have been an additional humiliation for the youngster now officially identified as a scapegrace. Perhaps even more difficult was presenting himself at Commodore Smith's home. The old commodore had cautioned Will about his behavior and no doubt felt a degree of humiliation that his young relative had betrayed his sponsorship and the uniform Smith had worn proudly for more than fifty years. It seems unlikely that Smith commiserated with Will. Whether he berated him or merely turned a cold shoulder on Will we do not know. Smith was a kindly man, and he would eventually write Welles on Will's behalf. But for some days Will wandered the streets of the capital without consolation.

He met classmates heading south and may have considered their arguments that he should join them. But Will was a devout Union man and refused. At the Navy Department, he met one of his former instructors, Lieutenant Charles W. Flusser, whom he held in high regard. The two talked frequently during the following days. Flusser, a Marylander, was unsure where his loyalties should lie and later credited Will with helping him choose to remain in the navy. He encouraged Will to seek reinstatement, however humiliating the conditions. At some point in these days both Flusser and Smith wrote Secretary Welles concerning Will's plight.

At 4:30 A.M. on April 12, 1861, Confederate guns opened fire on Fort Sumter in Charleston harbor. On hearing the news, Will went directly to the Navy Department to beg Welles for an appointment. The secretary was not indisposed to consider Will's case, but waited several days before summoning the young man for an answer. With an injunction about proper behavior, he handed Will an appointment as an acting master's mate, backdated to April 1. Will assured the secretary that he would not regret the kindness.

The appointment restored Will to the navy if not exactly to the status he would have enjoyed as a passed midshipman, the rank given to Naval Academy graduates until the rank of ensign was instituted in 1862. A master outranked a passed midshipman but an acting master fell a rung below in pay, prestige, and authority. Moreover, it was a rank that would soon be populated by a multitude of recent civilians, many of whom had never had a deck beneath their feet. But it was the navy, and Acting Master William B. Cushing would soon be at sea with an adventure to live and a reputation to win.

Coastal North Carolina, scene of Cushing's operations.
Battles and Leaders of the Civil War, The Century Co.: New York, 1884, Volume 4, p. 629.

The Sea Eagle

Early Duty and the Capture of Hatteras Inlet

I sailed from Boston in the Frigate *Minnesota* and reached Hampton Roads early in May of the year 1861.[1] The war had just commenced; the rebels had possession of Norfolk and were forming an army at Richmond.

When our ships with Admiral Stringham onboard came into the "Roads" we found at anchor the *Cumberland, Quaker City,* and *Monticello,* men of war. On our right hand was Fort Monroe, over which the old flag still waved, while five miles away, the sun shone upon a new banner raised in defiance—an emblem of treason. The *Monticello* (which I afterward commanded) had been in action with the battery on Sewell's Point, receiving several shots and losing a few men, gaining the honor of being the first ship under fire during the rebellion.[2]

We had been at anchor but a day when a fleet of five sail (schooners), loaded with tobacco came boldly down from Richmond. The South, in actual rebellion thought that none would dare molest them; and that a few of the chivalry[3] unarmed, ungrammatical and dirty, might under cover of the name "Virginian" pass through our fleet of "cringing Yankees" and proceed

---

[1]May 13, 1861.
[2]May 10, 1861. The claim, repeated elsewhere, is doubtful. The tug *Yankee* had exchanged fire with guns on Gloucester Point the day before the *Monticello's* action. Probably the best claim can be made on behalf of the chartered steamer *Star of the West*, which was fired on by Confederate batteries in Charleston while attempting to reach Fort Sumter on January 9, 1861.
[3]A frequent sarcastic labeling of Southerners, particularly the southern aristocracy.

upon their way, to exchange the fragrant weed for powder and shot that were required for our slaughter.

It is needless to say that we captured them all and that night I was sailing away for Philadelphia in the prize *Delaware Farmer*. After a narrow escape, in our crazy craft, during a gale of wind, I came to anchor in port, turned over the first prize of the war to the authorities and at once returned to Fortress Monroe; only to be sent off again prize master of the bark *Pioneer* bound for New York.

Taking passage in June, in the Frigate *Colorado*, I proceeded to Charleston S.C. and went on board the *Wabash*, remaining nearly a month blockading in view of Fort Sumter. Some captures were made, after which I went up to Hampton Roads to rejoin the *Minnesota*. An expedition was fitted out in August to go up the Black River in Chesapeake Bay, to storm a battery and some vessels. I was sent in the first launch. We had but a slight skirmish, but burned a number of schooners. The next month the capture of the Hatteras Forts was projected.

On the 26th of August we left Hampton Roads in the Frigate *Minnesota*, Flagship, *Monticello* [and] *Harriet Lane*, men of war, and three steam transports, bound for Hatteras Inlet, to attack the rebel forts. At this time the Inlet sent forth swarms of small privateers, and furnished a convenient harbor for blockade runners and as the gate way to the large inland waters of the Sounds, was of great importance. Its capture being determined upon, Admiral Stringham was selected as the commander of the expedition, and entrusted with the largest fleet that had, then, ever sailed in company under the American flag. We came in sight of the forts in the evening of the 27th and on the morning of the 28th, by the aid of surf boats succeeded in landing the few hundreds of soldiers, who under command of Gen. Butler, accompanied us. These took position two miles North of the enemy, and were joined by the marines of the squadron led by old Major Shuttleworth, who full of pluck, aspired to carry his wig into an assault that might remind him of former experience in Mexico.

The batteries were earthworks, two in number—and respectively named Fort Hatteras and Fort Clark and were commanded by Commodore Barron, rebel Flag Officer. At 10 o'clock, the squadron had moved into position in line, and the first gun was fired by the *Wabash*, answered by the rebel guns so promptly, that their shot seemed but our own rebounding. This was a great moment for me, a youngster who had never been fairly under fire—and I shall never forget or again experience the wild pleasure and excitement that I felt, as the stern challenge and response passed over the blue water on that sunny August day. I commanded the quarter deck division of eight 8-in. guns—and from my position upon deck had a fair view of every movement during the day. I was excited and eager—I was not so alone—I remember well our gallant old captain's look as the first whiz of rebel iron came to our ears.[4] With flushed face and sparkling eye he straightened his tall form, and with gray hair bared to the sun, stamped his foot upon the bridge and impulsively exclaimed—"Glorious! Glorious—Closer! Closer!"

We were soon in action—every ship a sheet of flame from bows to stern—and at 12:30 the flags from both forts were shot away and the enemy, in the act of abandoning Fort Clark, were rushing madly along the beach, while our shell tore through and through them—and bursting sent mangled bodies high in air, or buried them by dozens in sand graves upon the shore. At 2 P.M. the American colors were hoisted upon Fort Clark and no flag being displayed from the remaining fortification our Admiral concluded that it had surrendered, and ordered the *Monticello* to feel her way in, and gain its rear. Capt Ellis soon got aground in his attempt and the rebel guns suddenly opening fire, his vessel was in a critical situation. At least fourteen heavy guns were playing upon her at close range—but the *Monticello* promptly returned the fire; and at the same time coolly maneuvered to get out, which she succeeded in doing, in a somewhat shattered condition—covered in her retreat by the concentrated fire of the squadron. At sundown the fleet hauled off shore for the night, and we feared the morrow might prove stormy, in which case, the enemy might not only save their fort, but find our troops at their mercy. In consequence a spirit of gloom and doubt pervaded the squadron, that was not lifted until the bright sun and smooth sea of the 29th proved it good fighting weather and the signal was hoisted "All hands prepare for action."

At 8 A.M. we were again engaged, the enemy returning our fire in a spirited manner, but not again hoisting their flag after it was shot away early in the fight. The concentrated fire upon the fort was terrific—being mostly from one hundred and fifty-pounder guns fired with great care. Sixty shells exploded inside the parapets in a single minute—and at eleven o'clock an 11-in shell penetrated the bomb-proof[5] and entered the magazine—causing the immediate surrender.

A white flag was hoisted and a swarm of rebels appeared upon the fort, while at the same time signal was made to cease firing. Commodore Barron soon came over our side, and surrendered his sword upon the quarter deck—and we took possession of captured men and property—bringing the prisoners, some seven hundred and fifty in number on board the *Minnesota*.

---

[4]Captain Samuel Mercer.

[5]*bomb-proof*, a usually subterranean structure reinforced against artillery fire. Cushing uses the term to designate the mounded sand over the magazine.

An incident must be mentioned that professional men will appreciate. When it was ascertained that a 11 in shell had entered the ventilation of the enemy's magazine and thus forced a surrender—every officer in the fleet who commanded a gun of that calibre claimed the honor of the shot, and the dispute was both long and loud until it became known that the *fuse cap* had not been removed from the projectile—after which no claimant could be found—for no one would admit such a careless act as that of depriving the fuse of its effect.

The prisoners presented a curious and interesting appearance. They were not, in that early stage of the war content with the ordinary weapons of a soldier but were loaded down with bowie knives and revolvers each man a walking armory—evidently endeavoring to justify in dress the awe-inspiring titles they assumed—such as the "Lenoir Braves," the "Tar River Boys," "Hamilton Guards," and "Jonesboro Tigers"—these are a few of the ferocious company organizations that I remember which received the hospitality of the northern prisons as soon as we could take them to New York.

Our victory at Hatteras gave Gen. Butler his first public opportunity of showing the *modesty* for which he afterwards became so conspicuous by making speeches in which he implied that to him the credit of our action was due—whereas the affair was a purely Naval one—and General Butler's only part was in placing his name, with our Admiral's upon the articles of capitulation and accepting numerous serenades and dinners in the North for a merit which common decency should have forced on him to decline.

The Virginia Capes and the Battle of Hampton Roads

In Oct 1861 I was ordered to the *Cambridge*, a purchased screw vessel of about one thousand tons—where I did midshipman duty until the next March. During this time we blockaded in the Rappahannock River off Cape Henry; up the James and at Beaufort N.C. In the first named place I saw some sharp fighting in a cutting out expedition under the command of the gallant Lt. Wm. Gwin, afterwards killed in action on the Miss. River. He cut out a schooner, up a narrow stream, and was attacked by, and defeated a large force of infantry and artillery sent to take us. In a month we captured over four hundred negroes; or "contrabands" as they began to call them.

Off the Capes of Virginia my duty as boarding officer was very severe, as it was mid-winter, and I was frequently out in open boats for five and six hours at a time, with the icy sea and sleet dashing over me continually. Several times I was too stiff upon returning to step over the ships side and had to be hoisted on deck. This caused a sickness that sent me home and nearly cost me my life: but not before the famous *Merrimac[k]* fight—in which I had the honor to be under fire, and to lose a few drops of blood.

Our part in the action was to take in tow the sailing frigate *St. Lawrence*—and steam with her to where the *Congress* & *Cumberland* were maintaining an unequal contest with the iron clad and some consort steamers. Before we got under fire the *Cumberland* had gone down, hiding her crushed sides and bloody decks beneath the waters of the James—and a white flag at the mast head of the *Congress* told us that her fate was sealed, and that her brave commander, Joe Smith,[6] was no more.

The *Minnesota* which had preceded us, was aground desperately fighting her iron antagonist, whose shots tore through and through the wooden frigate at every moment. The *St. Lawrence* grounded under the fire of the Sewell's Point batteries, and we were soon warmly engaged with the heavy rifled guns of the enemy. With the *Merrimac* we exchanged a few shots just as she was withdrawing for the night. At eight in the evening we got the frigate afloat and anchored at Fortress Monroe preparing for a desperate and hopeless fight on the morrow. It seemed as if nothing could save our wooden fleet from utter destruction, as we were then virtually disabled; but the Providential arrival of the *Monitor* changed the aspect of affairs and we awaited the morrow with an eagerness amounting to impatience—a day big with the fate of future navies! The sun arose on a calm Sunday morning—and glistened on the side of the rebel monster—pressing boldly out in the early day, to finish the awful havoc that she had inaugurated.

The *Merrimac* steamed towards the *Minnesota* (still aground), preceded by the steamer *Yorktown*—scarcely noticing a black speck that moved out from behind our frigate—a something far from prepossessing in appearance and calculated to excite laughter, were it not that it bore the grand old flag, that would never have been risked to be disgraced. A Yankee hoax, said the enemy; and come on. Suddenly a puff of smoke rolled lazily from the *Monitor's* turret, and the leading vessel of the enemy turned and ran, like a beaten cur with a two hundred-pounder Yankee shell in her ribs, that had in some way been ejected from the "cheese box" with an aim and force that told of serious work ahead.

The two ironclads now went to work in earnest fighting at close quarters and exchanging iron blows that cracked sharp and distinct against adamantine sides, and sent the echo miles off amongst us spectators—riveting us with intense interest to the scene. It was settled at last, the dear old flag was safe and the national honor preserved—and even the sad fate of the *Cumberland* and

---

[6]Smith was Cushing's second cousin, the son of his mentor, Commodore Joseph Smith.

Congress did not stifle our rejoicing. The slaughter of Saturday was avenged by the victory of Sunday! Not a man had been killed upon the *Monitor*, but her brave Captain Worden was seriously wounded.

The day after this exciting duel we sailed to blockade the rebel steamer *Nashville*, then in the harbor of Beaufort, N.C. She escaped from us however, in the night our captain[7] refusing to permit me to enter the harbor and cut her out. He should have worn petticoats instead of the blue and gold of a dashing service—as his subsequent conduct proved when neglecting to face the enemy, he received from a Court Martial a sentence more merciful than just.

I was by this time, quite ill, and was sent home by a board of Medical Survey—but only remained ashore six weeks, before being ordered to the Frigate *Minnesota* again. After our capture of Norfolk, I went up the James River upon the staff of Admiral Goldsborough. It was just after the battle of Malvern Hill, and McClellan was anticipating a general engagement at Harrisons Landing. My brother[8] was on the staff of old Gen. Sumner, and when we met, I was so fired by his story of the Seven Days battle that I could not resist the temptation, in defiance of discipline of going on the same service in order to participate in the next affair. While ashore I rode on the staff of President Lincoln to review the army. Returning, disappointed in my warlike anticipations, to Norfolk, I was placed under suspension for leaving my Admiral. But as a midshipman is hardly considered a responsible being, was soon released.

Blackwater River

On July 16th 1862 I was promoted to the grade of Lieutenant, jumping the two commissioned grades of Master and Ensign—and ordered to report for duty in the Sounds of North Carolina. Here I became the executive officer of the U.S.S. *Commodore Perry* commanded by Lt Comdr Flusser for whose memory I have the greatest admiration. He was a man of clearest judgment, lion-like bravery, and pure patriotism. We became friends during a heavy fight up the Blackwater River—where he gave me the credit of saving the ship from boarders. The fight originated in a plan of Gen. Dix—who was to move on Franklin with twelve thousand men, while we took three vessels up the Blackwater to cut off the retreat of the seven thousand rebels to be attacked.

The army did not move—we were prompt—and at the time appointed found ourselves with two hundred men and fourteen cannon, fighting against all the enemy's force. The stream was very narrow and crooked and at the

---

[7]Commander William Parker.
[8]Alonzo Cushing.

bends we had to send lines ashore, making them fast to the trees to haul the ship's bows around.

Suddenly turning a point we came bows on to a barricade, formed by felling trees, from both banks, right across the stream. At the same time we drifted into the left bank. At once every tree, and bush and log sent forth a storm of lead—and a yell burst out that seemed to come from all directions.

We were in ambush—as it seemed madness to fight our few men in an open deck—Capt Flusser ordered all hands under cover. In a moment I looked over the side and saw a mass of infantry rushing to board us under cover of their comrades' fire.

Calling for volunteers I dashed out, cast loose the howitzer (on field carriage), and assisted by six men and an officer, Mr. Lynch, wheeled it to the other side of the deck. By that time I was again alone; all the volunteers

Lieutenant Commander Charles W. Flusser, one of Cushing's former instructors, became his mentor, captain, and friend.

Lieutenant Commander Charles W. Flusser, USN (1832–1864). Copy from a tintype taken at Plymouth, North Carolina, in 1864. Naval History and Heritage Command.

being dead or wounded at my feet. Without waiting an instant I sighted the piece, and sent the canister crashing amongst the dense mass, now about thirty yards away.

Its effect was fearful, and those who were not cut down became panic stricken and fell—all excepting the leader, a splendid looking fellow, with long curly hair—who came on, waving his sword; seemingly unconscious that he was alone. He met his death ten feet from our side. The men were now sent to quarters,[9] and a general fight commenced. The sailors working the great guns, throwing grape and canister; and our marines shielded by the hammocks,[10] picking the sharpshooters out of the tree tops—from whence they fell with a crash and shriek every moment. Our only hope was now to fight our way out—as no army force appeared to aid us—and six hours followed after the downward movement commenced—filled with attacks and repulses.

We were fighting to get possession of every bend, to send ashore our lines—the enemy striving in every way to keep us in the trap. Trees were cut down below us, forming barricades—and rifle pits were thrown up on every bluff and wooded point—But it was of no avail, Yankee mettle was not to succumb on that day. We butted through all obstructions, and made the rebs pay dearly for their sport. In going up stream our ship led the way; in returning the order was reversed the *Whitehead* being lowest down, followed by the *Hunchback* while the *Commodore Perry* brought up the rear, bloody and plucky. The leading vessels, rounding a bend, caught the fire of about a thousand infantry, concealed in a rifle pit—and after suffering severely ran by. We were some distance behind; and when we came around were entirely unexpected by the "butternuts,"[11] and were right on their flank and only two hundred yards distant. Instantly we threw a terrific fire of shrapnel, and grape shot through their trench till we could actually hear the bones crack, and see the limbs fly from the mangled bodies. In five minutes the place was in our possession and that of the dead.

At last, tired and feeble, we fired our last shot, and were clear once more, but with decks covered with the dead and wounded and slippery with blood—and the whole ship like a sieve, so full of bullet holes was she—but we had done our whole duty and could only regret that the Army failed us, and that our blue jackets had fallen in vain.

---

[9]*quarters*, fighting positions.

[10]During the day, hammocks were rolled and stored in racks along the rails, providing protection from small arms fire.

[11]Confederate infantrymen usually wore uniforms of butternut tan. Officers of high rank were frequently the only Confederate soldiers on a field of battle wearing regulation gray.

We afterwards heard that Gen. Dix had changed his plan and sent a streamer to notify us, but it had reached the "Sounds" a day too late.

Brave Flusser in his short and imperfect report has complimented me upon my conduct; and those who comprehend his character know what a compliment from him means. I am as proud of it as of any in the war.

Captain of the *Ellis* and the Battle of New River

I was now ordered to my first command—the gunboat *Ellis*—a captured rebel vessel. She was of iron, three eighths of an inch in thickness, measured about one hundred tons, and mounted an eighty-pounder rifle gun forward, and a 12-pdr rifle howitzer aft. As she drew but little water and could penetrate into every nook and corner, I was of course, delighted, and made up my mind to gain distinction or an honorable grave, before many months should go by.

The time soon came. Bogue Inlet is an opening into the ocean about thirty miles south of Beaufort. The bar is shallow, the breakers usually high, a tall bluff guards the entrance, and the little town of Swansboro nestles in the rear, about three miles from the mouth. It having been reported to the government that blockade running was carried on here, by means of small schooners to Nassau, I was ordered down the coast to look into the matter. After a slight skirmish I captured the town, procured provisions for my men and anchored to await events, but soon learning the rumor of traffic was false, I started down to the southard, without orders intending to have a look into some other inlets.

We dashed into New Topsail Inlet—twelve miles from Wilmington. We captured the schooner *Adelaide* with one hundred thousand dollars worth of cotton and spirits of turpentine on board. She was just about to sail for Bermuda. I was forced to burn her. I soon returned to Beaufort and reported that I had acted without orders, but was complimented highly, and ordered to continue on the coast where I used to coal at Beaufort; and start out upon expeditions in all directions.

Within a week of the destruction of the *Adelaide* I had again attacked the same Inlet—and after a sharp fight with some artillery, succeeded in destroying some large salt works, which were of great value; salt being very scarce in the South. In looking at the coast chart—my eye fell upon New River which empties into the Atlantic about forty miles below Beaufort N.C. I observed that it was wide and deep after the bar was crossed, and that the county seat called Onslow Court House adorned its banks about twenty miles from its mouth. In fact it seemed to me just the place for a nest of Nassau vessels and I determined to make a dash for it.

The following is my official account of the loss of the *Ellis* and of my operations in New River—with the endorsements of my Senior Officer and Admiral after a proper investigation. The Court Martial was denied me—Mr. Fox[12] saying "We don't care for the loss of a vessel, when fought as gallantly as that."

U.S.S. *Hetzel*
Off Newbern N.C.
November 27th 1862.

Sir:

I have the honor to enclose herewith a report of Lieutenant W. B. Cushing of his operations in New River Inlet, by which you will perceive that the U.S. Str [steamer] *Ellis* is lost. I trust that in consideration of the courage, coolness and gallantry displayed on the occasion by Lieut. Cushing, his course may meet with the approval of yourself and the Hon. Secretary of the Navy.

I have the honor to be—Very Respectfully
Your obt. Servt.
H. N. Davenport
Comdr & Senior Officer in Sounds of N.C.
[To] Rear Admiral
S. P. Lee
Comdg North Atlantic Squadron

(Indorsed)
Heartily approved and forwarded.
S. P. Lee, Rear Admiral

U.S.S. *Hetzel*
Nov 26th 1862

Sir:

I have the honor to report that I entered New River Inlet on the 23rd of this month with the United States Steamer *Ellis* under my command—succeeded in passing the narrow and shallow place called the Rocks, and started up the River. My object was to sweep the river, capture any vessels there, capture the town of Jacksonville, or Onslow Court House, take the Wilmington mail, and destroy any salt works that I might find on the banks. I expected to surprise the enemy in going up and there to fight my way out. Five miles from the mouth I came in sight of a vessel bound outward with a load of cotton and turpentine. The enemy fired her to prevent her falling into our hands. I ran alongside, made sure that

---

[12]Assistant Secretary of the Navy Gustavus Fox.

they could not extinguish the flames, and again steamed up the River. At 1 P.M. I reached the town of Jacksonville, landed, threw out my pickets and placed guards over the public buildings. This place is the county seat of Onslow County, and quite an important town. It is situated on the right bank of the river going up, and is thirty-five or forty miles from the mouth. I captured twenty-five stand of public arms in the Court House and Post Office, quite a large mail, and two schooners.

I also confiscated the negroes of the Confederate Post Master. I forgot to mention that the town is situated upon the main turnpike road from Wilmington. Several rebel officers escaped as I neared the town and carried the news to that city. At 2:20 P.M. I started down the river, and at 5 P.M. came in sight of a camp on the bank, which I thoroughly shelled. At the point where the schooner, captured in the morning was still burning, the enemy opened fire on the *Ellis* with rifles; but were soon silenced by our guns. I had two pilots on board, both of whom informed me that it would be impossible to take the steamer from the river that night.

High water and daylight were two things absolutely essential in order to take her out. I therefore came to anchor about five miles from the outer bar, took my prizes alongside, and made every preparation to repel an attack. All night long the signal fires of the enemy could be seen upon the banks. At daylight I got underway and had nearly reached the worst place in the channel, when the enemy opened on us with two pieces of artillery. I placed the vessel in position, at once hoisted the battle flag at the fore, the crew gave it three cheers, and we went into action. In one hour we had driven the enemy from his guns and from the bluff and passed within a hundred yards of their position without receiving fire. Up to this time I had been in every way successful, but was here destined to meet with an accident that changed the fortunes of the day and resulted in the destruction of my vessel. About five hundred yards from the bluffs, the pilots, mistaking the channel, ran the *Ellis* hard and fast aground.

All hands went to work, at once, to lighten her, and anchors and steam were used to get her afloat, but without success. The headway of the steamer had forced her over a shoal, and into a position where as the center of a circle, we had a circumference of shoal all around. When the tide fell I sent a party ashore to take possession of the artillery abandoned in the morning; but when they reached the field it was discovered that it had [been] removed while we were at work upon the vessel.

If I had secured this I proposed to construct a shore battery to assist in the defense of my vessel, by keeping the rebels from placing their battery in position. At dark I took one of my prize schooners alongside and proceeded to take everything out of the *Ellis* excepting the pivot gun, some ammunition, two tons of coal and a few small arms. Steam and anchor again failed to get my vessel afloat. I felt confident that the confederates would come on me in overwhelming force, and it now became my duty to save my men. So all hands were called to muster, and the crew told that they [should] go aboard the schooners.

I called for six volunteers to remain with me on board and fight the remaining gun. Knowing that it was almost certain death the men came forward, and two Masters Mates Valentine and Barton were amongst the number. These gentlemen subsequently behaved with coolness and bravery.

I ordered the schooner to drop down the channel out of range from the bluffs and there to wait for the termination of the impending engagement, and if we were destroyed to proceed to sea. Early in the morning the enemy opened upon us from four points with heavy rifled guns (one a Whitworth).[13] It was a cross fire and very destructive. I replied as best I could, but in a short time the engine was disabled, and she was much cut up in every part, and the only alternatives left were surrender or a pull of one and a half miles, under their fire, in my small boat. The first of these was not, of course, to be thought of, the second I resolved to attempt. I fired the *Ellis* in five places and having seen that the battle flag was still flying, trained the gun upon the enemy so that the vessel might fight herself after we had left—and started down the river, reached the schooner and made sail for sea. It was low water on the bar and a heavy surf was rolling in, but the wind forced us through after striking several times. We were just in time, for about six hundred yards down the beach were several companies of cavalry trying to reach the mouth of the inlet in time to cut us off. We hoisted our flag, gave three cheers and were off. In four hours I reached Beaufort. I brought away all my men, rifled howitzer and ammunition, the ship's stores and clothing, the men's bags and hammocks, and a portion of the small arms. I retained on board the *Ellis* a few muskets, pikes and pistols to repel boarders. I neglected to state that when I took possession of the enemy's ground on the 24th—a salt work was destroyed, and ten boats rendered useless that were to have been used for boarding.

At 9 a.m. the United States Steamer *Ellis* was blown in pieces by the explosion of the magazine.

Officers and men behaved nobly, obeying orders strictly under the most trying circumstances.

I respectfully request that a Court of Inquiry may be ordered to investigate the facts of the case, and to see if the honor of the flag has suffered in my hands.

I am Sir, Very Respectfully
Your Obedient Servant
Wm B. Cushing
Lieutenant

(Indorsed)
Commander H. N. Davenport

---

[13]*Whitworth*, a rifled breach-loader imported from Great Britain by the Confederacy. Generally considered the most accurate artillery design of the war.

Senior Officer & C.V.C.
Respectfully submitted—I think the course of this young officer should meet
with the commendation of his superiors.
H. N. Davenport
Commander & Senior Officer
(Further indorsed)
Received and forwarded Dec 2nd 1862 with the expression of my admiration
for Lieutenant Cushing's coolness courage and conduct.
S.P. Lee
Rear Admiral
[To] Hon Gideon Welles
Sec of the Navy

*Secretary of the Navy Gideon Welles (1802–1878) became
Cushing's most influential supporter.*
Library of Congress.

Little River

After my return to Newbern [New Bern] from this expedition I received from Major General Foster Commdg the Department of North Carolina a letter complimenting me on my action—and with it a copy of a letter to Admiral Lee—in which the general requested that I might be detailed to command a squadron of five army steam gun boats to co-operate with his forces. As I was but nineteen years of age at the time I thought and still think this a high endorsement of my conduct in command, but I did not second the application, for the reason that I did not wish to relinquish actual Naval Service and desired one vessel of the Navy more than a fleet of army boats. I will only add that as my magazine in the *Ellis* was entirely exposed those who volunteered to remain with me and fight for the honor of the flag, deserve great credit.

After escaping in my captured prize to Beaufort I went to Newbern and was for some weeks off duty; but was soon to indulge in an adventure which for real peril and excitement is equal to any. At this time the government was meditating an attack upon Wilmington, but was in want of some good pilots for that harbor. These I proposed to capture and receiving permission, I fitted out a little prize schooner of mine; disguising her as English. My plan was to run boldly in under the forts, take pilot on board, and run out, trusting to the boldness of the affair to carry me clear. But at both the east and west bars of that harbor, I was becalmed so that I was seen by the enemy in the midst of our men of war. I was therefore obliged to change my views. Learning that there was a pilot station up Little River just at the boundary between North and South Carolina, I suddenly dashed in at night, during the month of February 1863. The stream was narrow and with wooded banks. About two miles up, I caught sight of a flag staff, on a bluff, in relief against the sky, and at the same instant received a volley of musketry. I had but twenty men, in three small boats, and several were at once knocked over, but I saw that decisive action was required, if any were to be saved.

Instantly I sprang up in my boat, and sang out "Follow me in!" turning the boats' bows at the same time inshore. In a moment I had the men up the bluff and ordered them to charge, in a loud voice. At the enemy we went, yelling like demons—and coming out into an open space saw, by the light of a camp fire, an earth work looming up in front. It was no time to turn back—another yell and we were through the ditch and over the parapet, sole possessors of a fort and blockhouse from which the frightened garrison five times our number, had run away, deceived by our boldness into the belief that they, not we were the surprised party. They left their arms, clothes &c as the spoils of war, and a supper of pork and greens upon the table; to which our tired jack tars did full justice, winding up the meal by a fight with the returned chivalry, and the destruction of everything valuable that we could not take away. The next morning found us still at anchor off the river; our little craft riding to a heavy swell that came rolling in from the southard and westard.

Every thing denoted a coming storm and nothing could be more unfortunate for us. Cape Fear and Frying Pan shoals make out into the sea a distance of thirty miles, forming with the coast a right angle into which bight, a S. W. gale blows direct—making an awful sea, and at that time, a rebel lee shore. And it was just in that bight that I found myself, in a centre-board schooner of forty tons, with but one anchor and fifteen fathoms of chain. It soon came in to blow a heavy gale, and though I managed to keep close reefed canvas upon the little *Hope*, I soon found that there was no chance of weathering the Frying-pan. She went to leeward as rapidly as ahead. A thick fog now came to add to our perplexity—so dense that the water was not visible at more than two hundred yards distance; but the rain that came with it served to beat down, in a measure the immense sea.

I now had my choice of two alternatives either of which were not pleasant. I might bear up for the beach and go ashore at Fort Caswell, as a prisoner of war—and join our poor fellows in the Hell of Andersonville[14]—or I might run the thirty miles that separated us from the shoal—calculating the lee-way made and run the chance of striking a narrow channel that runs like a thread across it. Even there I knew it must be breaking and I do not exaggerate when I say that the chances were five hundred to one against us. If we missed our way by a hundred yards in the fog, there was a certainty that we would be dashed in pieces. Nevertheless I decided upon this last named course—let but one man know the danger—Mr. Valentine—a Masters Mate—placed him at the helm with instructions how to act and gave the compass course that I decided upon.

The gale increased in violence, as time wore slowly by and the moment drew near when our fate would be decided. All at once I saw the old quartermaster at the lead[15] turn deathly pale as he sang out "Breakers ahead! For God's sake, sir, go about." In an instant the cry was "Breakers ahead on the bow! Breakers on the weather bow!" And we were into them. All seemed over now, but we stood at the helm, determined to control our boat to the last. A shock—she had struck—but it was only for a second and she still fairly flew through the great white breakers.

---

[14]Writing after the war, Cushing was guilty of an anachronism. The Andersonville prison camp was not established until February 1864.

[15]lead, a weight on a marked line thrown from the bow to measure the depth of water.

Cushing distinguished himself as executive officer of the USS Commodore Perry under the command of his friend Charles Flusser. Later Cushing would command the USS Commodore Barney, a similar converted ferry.

Records of the Office of the Chief Signal Officer, 1860–1982; National Archives.

Again and again she struck, but never hard—she had found the channel, and in twenty minutes we were safe, and scudding for Beaufort.

The next morning I was ashore again and not, thank God, on traitors ground.

Nansemond River

I now proceeded to Hampton Roads to take command of the steamer *Commodore Barney* a vessel mounting five one-hundred pounder smooth bore guns, a one-hundred pounder Parrot rifle and a twelve-pound howitzer: she carried a crew of one hundred and fifty men. I was at this time offered command of the *Violet*, a fast boat intended for capture of prizes off Wilmington, but as there was a good appearance of coming war about Norfolk I declined. I was soon rewarded. Longstreet besieged Suffolk in April and endeavored to outflank Gen. Peck, and throw his army between our force and Norfolk. To prevent this it was necessary to hold the narrow stream called Nansemond River and I was selected by the admiral for the undertaking. Lieut. Lamson was in the river when I assumed command[16] with the light steamers *Mount Washington* and *Stepping Stones*. I took with me besides my ship the tug boat *Cohasset*. The army gunboat *West End* was also in the stream. On the 14th, as Lamson was bringing his ships down to join me—the *Mount Washington* grounded less than 100 yards from a bluff—Hills Point and about three hundred from where I was anchored. The enemy at once unmasked a battery of rifled guns which were stationed in a sunken earth work on the point; and a fight commenced that was both stubborn and bloody.

The army boat soon deserted me and I sent the tug down to watch the fords below.

Lamson was soon badly cut up, but fought with the pluck of a hero against what seemed a fated destruction. With the rising tide I pulled aboard his ship in my gig, and took the bearings of affairs—and as soon as she would float, ordered the little *Stepping Stones* to take her in tow and run for it. In the mean time the battle was exceedingly warm, as we were never more than three hundred yards from the muzzles of the rebel guns, and were also under the

---

[16]Cushing was senior to Lamson and technically in command when their ships were in company. However, the *Barney* could not penetrate the upper Nansemond because of her draft, and Lamson operated independently in that part of the river through almost the entire campaign. Admiral Lee seems to have considered it a joint command. Lamson sent his reports directly to Lee without endorsement by Cushing. Frequently the two sent joint reports and received joint orders from Lee. It is hard to avoid the conclusion that Cushing was exaggerating his responsibility at this point in his memoir.

fire of musketry. After five hours of this work the *Stepping Stones* went down stream with Mt. *Washington* in tow; the last named vessel a wreck, with over a hundred shot holes in her, but flying the stars and stripes from a staff that had been thrice cut away, and thrice lashed up again by gallant Lamson.

The *Barney* was now left alone and in an hour more had silenced the opposing guns and anchored with a loss of many [of] her crew, two guns disabled, and badly cut up fore and after. This was certainly a tough fight. For three weeks we fought daily and were never beaten.

The steamers *Yankee*, *Coeur-de-Leo* & *Primrose* meanwhile reported to me for duty; and took part in the sport. In the contest I met as enemies one who was a classmate at Annapolis and one cousin both of whom it gave me much satisfaction to defeat. One night our sailors, in conjunction with an army detachment, stormed and captured the sunken earth work in our front, bringing off six captured cannon. The credit of this was mainly due to Lamson. Another day I landed with ninety sailors and a howitzer—marched inland and captured the town of Chuckatuck, four hours after it had been the head quarters of Longstreet's left wing. This proved a very important reconnaissance as it demonstrated that the rebel flanking force had drawn back; and therefore that their main body was moving away to reinforce Lee for the expected battle with Hooker's force.[17]

A circumstance of my raid, which at the time furnished much amusement to our army, is worth relating. After driving in the cavalry pickets of the enemy, I ambushed half of the men at some cross roads to protect my rear, and then advanced towards the town. Having captured a cart, drawn by two mules, I converted it into a limber; placing my ammunition inside and making fast the trail rope of the howitzer to the rear. We could then advance at the double quick. As we entered the streets of the town, a rebel cavalry company came charging around the corner, two hundred yards away, with drawn sabres and horses at the gallop. I instantly unlimbered and blazed away, but the shrapnel just went over them and burst in their rear. At the sound of the gun the mules dashed off at a run—right against the advancing cavalry, with the old cart swinging first to one side and then to the other of the road. Mules and cavalry came in contact in the narrow street, and great confusion ensued.

"Load with canister!" said I.

"All gone in the mule cart!" was the answer. Sure enough! It was all gone, and I had not an ounce of ammunition. Something had to be done—so I ordered a charge and the novel sight ensued of sailors charging and beating

---

[17]The Battle of Chancellorsville, May 1–4, 1863. Longstreet did not arrive in time for the battle.

cavalry. We killed a number, recaptured our cart, took the town, and several of the enemies' horses all equipped, with pistols at the saddle bows. After mounting the officers, a fine horse remained that I desired to save—so I shipped an old tar on his back and we started to return.

In going through some woods we were attacked when I again made use of my howitzer, which had the same effect on the old sailor's animal that it had previously on the mules—he went about and shaped a course right back for town.

Jack[18] saw that he was struck by a squall, and tried to luff[19]—but it was of no use—and as for anchoring it was just out of the question. But discipline in the school of danger now came to his assistance. Quickly pulling out one of the pistols from the holsters, he placed the muzzle at the horse's ear and blazed away. The speed of the runaway was great, so that it took about a dozen bounds, end over end to satisfy his momentum, and our jolly "shellback"[20] found himself seated in a ditch, with the wreck alongside.

Stripping the rigging off he came in to join us, with the saddle on his back, swearing against a craft that wouldn't answer its helm.

While engaged one morning with two batteries: my bow guns with one a quarter of a mile away, and the broadside against another in Lecount's Hill twelve hundred yards distant, I had a narrow escape. In the woods on the enemies' bank, I had stationed five men, who were ordered to conceal themselves and keep a bright lookout. If the infantry came down upon us they were to fire once and retreat under the bluff—and I had two heavy guns loaded with grape to meet such an emergency. As our ship in her movements neared the woods, I saw one man under the bank, at the waters edge, waving his hat as if to warn us back; but as no musket had been fired, and he was not twenty yards away, I sang out to him in an angry tone to know what it meant. As I hailed, a crashing volley of musketry came from amongst the trees, and there was no need of further inquiry.

I was standing in bold relief on the hurricane deck and was in full uniform, with speaking trumpet and marine glass in hand; yet I escaped without injury. Three buckshot penetrated my clothing to the skin; and my hair at the crown of head was cut off close to the scalp. Ten minutes served to satisfy the ardor of the attacking party—who could not face nine-inch grape—but they left some of our best men dead on our deck. It seems that Longstreet's

---

[18]*Jack* or *Jack Tar*, traditional slang for a sailor in the age of sail.

[19]*luff*, to turn the bow into the wind, a maneuver to minimize the surface area exposed to a high wind that might heel a ship dangerously over on its side.

[20]*shellback*, a traditional slang term for a veteran sailor, mildly pejorative, implying a reluctance to abandon traditional methods in the face of new circumstances.

men made their way through a point of swamp and came on my pickets so suddenly that there was no time to alarm us in the matter indicated, but this one brave sailor, placed himself right beneath the muzzles of their rifles and tried to warn me.

As soon as the firing commenced he jumped into a boat on the beach, sculled off a short distance, took up his rifle and fired; a few yards further on he loaded and fired again, and continued to fight in that way until the confederates withdrew.

Strange to say he was not hit; though the boat in which he escaped was riddled by sixty balls. Such contests as the one described above took place frequently during the siege; as the presence of our light vessels in so small a stream, was a constant challenge, which a gallant enemy would not decline.

In this campaign, it is my opinion that very bad generalship was shown by the commanding officer of our army in Suffolk—Gen Peck. When I found that Longstreet's left wing, or flanking, force had fallen back, I at once concluded that his main force was moving to join Lee: because it must either be so moving, or massing upon a front for assault, where they knew defeat to be certain.

That Longstreet knew Peck's defenses and numbers I cannot doubt; for I captured an engineer officer of his force, with the plans of our works, their names, and the number and position of our men in his possession, and it was mere madness, with such information to think of storming our front. They must then have been in retreat; leaving but two or three thousand men to amuse our general; and it was with this information that I rode nine miles in a dark night and drenching rain to urge an advance of our forces. I wrote to Admiral Lee at the same time, the state of the case—and did not hesitate to say that Peck had it in his power to either capture what men remained, or keep Longstreet's main body north of the Blackwater.

But the general was convinced that the army was massing on his front, and did not advance for a week—when as I predicted, a mere shell was found—a skirmish line—that went off like a puff of smoke before our regiments.

Admiral S. D. Lee will remember how constantly I urged my opinion in regard to Longstreet's strategy—and he, at the time, agreed with me in thinking Peck too timid for the public good. At the close of our duty in [the] Nansemond I received from the Secretary of the Navy a letter of congratulation and thanks. My vessel was so badly cut up as to need repairs at some navy yard, and we were ordered to Baltimore, where in the course of six weeks she was again put in fighting trim.

In the meantime I had the honor of being privately presented to President Lincoln and enjoyed keenly an hour's conversation with him. His Excellency was pleased to compliment me heartily upon my success.

Gettysburg

After doing duty for some time in the James River, my ship was ordered on an expedition up the York R. to White House. In this raid, near Richmond, Brigadier Gen [W. H. Fitzhugh "Rooney"] Lee, a son of Robert E. was captured. In June of 1863 the rebels advanced into Maryland, and Washington being threatened my command was ordered to the Capital to defend the City. Soon after my arrival the battle of Gettysburg took place.

In that action my Brother fell fighting most nobly, in command of Battery "H," 4th U.S. Artillery.[21]

I at once proceeded to the field, with the double purpose of securing his body; and, as all his officers were killed, of fighting his guns, if permitted to do so, in the next battle. The field, when I reached it was a sickening sight. Thirty thousand wounded men, and thousands of unburied dead lay on the earth—in road, field, wood and orchard and under the scorching sun on the bare hillside amidst all the wreck of a great battle. Dismounted cannon, dead horses, exploded caissons and broken muskets were everywhere—and the artillery position on Cemetery Hill was almost paved with the rebel iron that had been hurled by the hundred and fifty guns massed against it previous to the final charge.

My Brother's battery was destroyed. Five out of the six guns were dismounted—all the officers and most of the men were shot, and seventy of its horses stiffened upon the wooded knoll where they were placed for shelter. Our army had moved on in pursuit of the foe, and there was nothing left for me to do, but to return to naval duty.

As I write this, rocked on the long swell of the Pacific, under the warmth of an equatorial sun, my mind goes back in review of the many sad scenes in those bloody years of rebellion—but fails to bring up any picture that is so grand or solemn or mournful as that great theatre of death.

The wounds were not alone for those who fell upon the field. There is suffering greater than the dying know—the prolonged anguish of those left behind to mourn them.

Shokoken

In the month of August 1863, the steamer *Shokoken* was sent upon the blockade as an experiment of the Navy Department. She was a large and fast ferry-boat, with the hull built out, and, supposing her then to be seaworthy,

---

[21]Alonzo Cushing.

possessed many advantages in maneuvering amongst the shoals of Wilmington harbor.

Hardly had she joined the squadron on the coast, ere, without a trial, she was pronounced unseaworthy, and ordered by the Senior Officer to return to Hampton Roads. This did not suit the ideas of our Admiral, and, her commanding officer being relieved, I was ordered to her, and sent to sea. Now I had serious doubts as to whether she would survive a good stiff gale—but made up my mind to find out consoling myself with the philosophy of Bryan Bolin,[22] "that there's ground at the bottom." Within the first week we drove ashore the large blockade running steamer *Hebe*, while endeavoring to run in; and though prevented by a gale of wind from towing her off—succeeded in burning her after a sharp fight with a rebel battery of rifled guns.[23]

Two days after I discovered a vessel in New Topsail Inlet and requested permission to cut her out, but the Senior Officer declined to permit it upon the curious plea of "risk of life"—and responsibility.

I therefore determined to try it without permission. By sending in boats we discovered that a battery of six guns guarded the mouth—and that the distance to the wharf, at which our coveted prize was secured, was about six miles. Strategy was required to ensure success and avert blood-shed. I anchored the *Shokoken* close into the beach, about four miles to the northard of the mouth of the inlet, which position left me separated by about half a mile from the Sound inside—the intermediate land being covered with scrub oak. The enemy seeing us at anchor, concluded that a boat expedition was preparing, to go in at the mouth of the opening, and made every preparation for our reception.

One gun, with twenty men and the captain, went up to the wharf, where the piece was pointed to rake the deck of their vessel—the other guns were left, ready to blow us out of the water, in their original position. Then men were posted at the mast heads of their craft, and all was deemed secure.

Night came; and so did the Yankees. Instead of going in at the mouth of the inlet; I took ashore, four miles above it, two boat's crews, made them shoulder the dingy (a very small boat) and carry it across the neck of land;

---

[22]*Bryan Bolin.* I have been unable to find a reference to a character real or fictional of this name. The word *bolin* is a variant spelling of *bowline*, a common sailor's knot. Hence, *Bryan Bolin* might have been a slang term for a fatalistic "old salt." I have not, however, found any substantiation for this theory.

[23]Cushing may have overstated his role. According to *Lincoln's Commando*, the blockader *Niphon* had already driven the *Hebe* ashore at the time Cushing and the *Shokoken* arrived on the scene. However, the *Niphon's* boarding party had wrecked its boat in the gale and was stranded aboard the grounded *Hebe* and under attack from Confederate cavalry. *Niphon* and *Shokoken* sent additional boats but were unable to accomplish a rescue. The stranded sailors surrendered and *Niphon* and *Shokoken* set the *Hebe* ablaze with gunfire.

launching it in the reeds, two miles from the blockade runner and in a position entirely outflanking the main battery. To shorten the story—we surprised and charged in the night, with six sailors, the force guarding the schooner,[24] routed them—took their artillery, and ten prisoners, including the captain—burned the vessel and destroyed some large salt works. In doing this two men were thrown out as pickets, two guarded the prisoners, and two, assisted by the plantation darkies, burned the vessel and buildings. The prisoners proved "an elephant" in our hands for the dingy was entirely too small to bring them off, and it was impossible to guard them in moving through the thick brush in the darkness. A great show of orders was therefore made to imaginary boats off upon the water, and ordering three of the prisoners into the dingy, to be there to receive them. The rest were instructed to go a quarter of a mile up the bank and report to a "Lt. Jones" who was supposed to be there to receive them. They were cautioned not to go too far out, or our pickets might shoot them, and went off without an idea of the smallness of our force, or our inability to take them with us.

The next morning upon coming in sight of the squadron, I found them in by the beach engaging a battery, which was situated near the wreck of the *Hebe*. Knowing the water well, I got a position close in, and proceeded to serve out grape and canister but becoming impatient, hoisted signal for permission to board. Not receiving an answer I went on board the Admiral's ship, and asked permission to take the guns by storm. This proposition was declined as it was intended to shell them a while longer, and then to land two hundred sailors and marines to cut the enemy off. But to be within grape range and not act was too much for my patience. I lowered two boats upon the side away from the enemy—took twenty men and in a moment dashed around the stem and ashore. We took two rifled pieces—one a Whitworth— and when assistance came from the Flag Ship, got them off [to] my vessel.

I never was credited officially with this—perhaps because I disobeyed orders, or, maybe, for the reason that the great fish present could not surrender so dainty a morsel to "a youngster." Shortly after this we were caught in a very heavy north east gale, and were nearly lost. All the ships had to run to sea, and my only chance was to get around the shoal under the lee of Smiths Island. This I succeeded in doing—but only when my sponsons[25] were knocked away— decks raised, and boiler wrenched from the hull by the storm. It was close work and quite experiment enough. So thought Admiral Lee, who believed us under water, until we steamed to meet him upon his return two days after.

---

[24]According to Naval Records, the vessel was the *Alexander Cooper*.
[25]*sponsons*. Air-filled tanks along the hull intended to give a vessel greater stability.

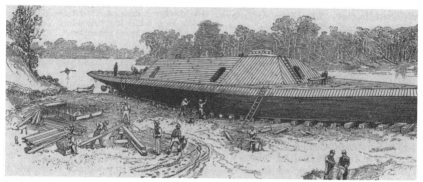

By the late summer of 1863, when Cushing took command of the Monticello, *the ironclad ram C.S.S.* Albemarle *was well on the way to completion at Edward's Ferry, sixty miles up the Roanoke from Union-occupied Plymouth.*
Battles and Leaders of the Civil War, *The Century Co.: New York, 1884, Volume 4, p. 626.*

Monticello

I was detached from the *Shokoken* and ordered to Washington as bearer of dispatches. That I was not forgotten in these, I judge from the fact, that I was ordered to command the *Monticello*—then fitting out in Philadelphia— Mr. Fox saying—"You are ordered to this command for distinguished services rendered."

I was now ashore for some months, superintending the outfit of my vessel. The times were decidedly squally—the electioneering feeling in Pennsylvania running very high. I was glad enough to get to sea again after being placed in "durance vile"[26] for thrashing a few copperheads who insulted me, for no other reason than because I wore the uniform of my country's navy. In February 1864, I was off Wilmington blockading. In the day time we had stations for anchoring, out of range of the enemy's shot. In the night each ship crept close in lining the bar—the lead colored hulls blending in with fog and foam—and every eye alert to catch sight of an entering or escaping steamer. Great care was required not to run ashore, and to avoid being disabled by the rebel fire when the moon came out [and] found us close under a hundred of their cannon.

I was forced to get all the sleep that I required during the fore-noon— never at night. They had a practice ashore of trying to disable us by pointing a number of guns with different elevations in the same plane of fire—so that when all were fired one was apt to take effect. Besides the line of ships close in there was a squadron in position well off from the coast. It was the duty of

---

[26]Cushing was arrested by the local police and spent the night in jail.

these cruisers to calculate for "moon and tide," the time that a steamer would be most likely to escape from the harbor and, supposing her to make, through the night, a certain number of knots speed—place themselves where they would probably sight the black smoke in the morning. The lookout at the mast heads commanded a horizon of some fifteen miles, and many a steamer was so seen and captured. As the sun commenced to light up the ocean the hail would come from aloft—"Black smoke, sir!" "Where away?" "Two points on the port bow sir!" and the exciting chase would commence.

It was exciting. Sometimes a few hours sufficed in which to overhaul the lead colored fugitive—often darkness would terminate an unsuccessful chase—and our blue jackets would have to console themselves by the saying that "there are as good fish in the sea as ever were caught"—a poor substitute for the half million dollars that had run away from them during the day. In many of these races the runner when hard pressed, would throw overboard her deck load of cotton, and it was not an uncommon thing to see a hundred thousand dollars worth of the "royal staple" floating unheeded, by.

On the night of the 22nd of February the *Monticello* was inshore, off Fort Caswell and I made up my mind that the birthday of Washington was entitled to a celebration. I therefore muffled the oars of three of our boats, and with forty men, succeeded in passing in between the forts, into the harbor.

My object was to find a prize inside; capture her by boarding, and run her out, by their guns, to our squadron. There were no vessels at the anchorage so, I thought of dashing into a heavy battery on Smiths Island and bringing off its flag. Pulling in with my gig to reconnoiter, I found that when my oars grazed the face of the work I was not challenged. The rebels felt perfectly secure and had grown careless. As my force was small I determined to give no alarm but to get reinforcements from the squadron, and with the Senior Officer's permission take and *hold* the island until relieved by the army force. Such an event would have closed to the enemy one of the troublesome entrances to Cape Fear River. I could have affected this result with two hundred men; but as usual met the reply to my proposal—"Can't take the responsibility." This, I confess provoked me—and I told the Senior Officer that I could not only do that; but if he wanted the Confederate General off to breakfast I would bring him. I then left, and went to my ship.

That night I took twenty men, pulled by the forts and straight up the river to the town of Smithville, the rebel head-quarters. I knew nothing of it excepting that fact, and its position on the chart; but my plan was too bold to fail. I succeeded in landing right in front of the hotel not thirty yards from the angle of the fort, in the centre of the town, and hid my men under the bluff. We then crept down to a salt work on the point and captured two darkies who were there at work—thus gaining what information I desired. My object was to take the Commanding General[27] from his bed, in the midst of his men and to take him out of the harbor in one of his own steamers. But alas! no steamer was there. Leaving most of the sailors in ambush I crept up the street with the negro guide and two of my officers, soon reaching a large house with the southern veranda—the general's residence.

It was directly opposite the barracks in which twelve hundred men were sleeping—and not fifty feet from them. Gaining the door I opened it and proceeded to explore—finding first a mess room, then some stairs up which I made my way. Lighting a match at the top I saw some doors and had just opened one of them when I heard a crash below, and my officers' voices saying "Captain! Captain!" Down I went, and opened a door below—striking a match at the same time, and by the flash, I saw a man in dishabille with a chair in hand as if to strike. Dashing in at once I had him on his back in an instant, with the muzzle of a revolver at his temple, and my hand on his throat. I doubted not but that my prize was the dignitary sought. Threatening to kill him if he spoke, I struck another match and lit the candle. I then found that it was the Chief Engineer of the defenses that I had, and that the general was away in Wilmington. Besides this misfortune—the Adjutant General had just escaped from the house. It seems that his bed was close to the window and hearing a noise, he arose and looked out. The first sight that met his eye was the muzzle of a navy revolver about two inches from his nose. Down went the window with a crash and the fearfully demoralized officer wrenching his arm through—dashed out the back door—in garments hardly fitted for display. It was a good joke but not exactly the time for me to laugh at it, as I knew that soldiers would swarm out like angry bees in a minute. So I hurried my prisoner into his most necessary garments, pocketed the papers of the absconding adjutant and hastened down to my boat. The town was alive by this time but like the old gent with the spectacles on his forehead—looking everywhere but in the right place.

I shoved off with officer and contrabands, and was nearly down to fort Caswell before the signal lights told the sentinel forts that Yankee boats were in the harbor—and while the long roll was beating there, and "butternuts" rushing to their guns—I quietly pulled through the opening and off to my ship. It was twelve o'clock at night when I entered the Head Quarters—and moon light—at one, I was in my cabin, had given my rebel dry socks and a glass of sherry, laughed at him, and put him to bed.

---

[27]The intended victim of Cushing's exploit was Brigadier General Louis Hébert (West Point, 1845).

The swift blockade-runner A. D. Vance *plied the run between Wilmington and Bermuda. Captured, she became the blockader* Advance, *although some, like Cushing, continued to use her former name.*

The photographic history of the civil war . . . Francis Trevelyan Miller, editor-in-chief; Robert S. Lanier, managing editor. *Thousands of scenes photographed 1861–65, with text by many special authorities.* Publisher: New York, The Review of Reviews Co., 1911–12.

The next morning to the astonishment of the Senior Officer I took my guest off to breakfast and requested permission to send in a flag of truce for his clothes and some money. My boat was permitted to land on the beach and the officer whom I sent in was met as he went ashore by Col. Jones, the commander of Fort Caswell. My officer's name was Jones also and he had been with me [the] night before. Both of these gentlemen were on their extreme dignity; the colonel saying that he would telegraph up to Smithville and see if he could receive the flag of truce.

They walked up and down the beach in silence and passed each other several times, when the rebel wheeled sharply and suddenly round and exclaimed "That was a d—d splendid affair, Sir." This broke the ice, and a chat ensued; soon joined in by the Adjutant General, with arm in a sling, and limping from the effects of his impromptu promenade of the night before. My prisoner's clothes were sent for, and bacon and hard tack with which to regale their guest. A letter was now produced which I sent in for the General—It read as follows.

My Dear General,
    I deeply regret that you were not at home when I called. I enclose my card.

Very respectfully,
W. B. Cushing

This was unanimously declared the essence of impudence, but did not prevent them from sending me off the latest papers. They could not guess when I entered, or escaped from the harbor, as they said that thousands of eyes watched every square inch of it. The next day I started for Beaufort to coal and early in the morning ran into and sunk the U.S.S. *Peterhoff*; formerly the famous blockade runner. It was an unavoidable accident, arising from the strict rules of the blockade, that required instantaneous signals in order to avoid being fired into or run down. My false stem[28] was carried away and we proceeded to Norfolk for repairs.

Chasing the *Raleigh*

Returning to my coaling station at Beaufort in the month of June we heard that the iron clad *Raleigh* had been out amongst our fleet at Wilmington, escorting some blockade runners, at night, and remaining out until morning. Why she was not attacked I do not to this day know—but as soon as we heard the news, Lt Comdr Braine in the *Vicksburg* and myself in the *Monticello*, started down the coast, determined to ram her in company upon sight. In case she were inside I made out a written application and plan to take her by boarding in the harbor. I sent a copy of this to Admiral Lee at Hampton Roads, and took the other down to submit it to the Senior Officer. As usual, no one would take responsibility excepting myself. I argued that the noses of the squadron had virtually been pulled, and begged permission to go in—promising not to come out alive if I failed. It was of no use.

Capt Sands declined to give me the men—and it was not until some time after that I received a letter from Admiral Lee "heartily approving" my course, and permitting me to call upon the S. Offr. [Senior Officer] for such men and boats as I desired. It was disgraceful to delay it an hour! On the night of June 25th, with fifteen men and two officers, Howorth and Martin—I ran by forts Caswell, Holmes and the outer batteries guarding the harbor. With muffled oars, we proceeded up the stream, keeping a bright lookout for the iron-clad and for the guard boats. In passing the town of Smithville, I was nearly run down by a tug that passed on unsuspected. I was determined to find the *Raleigh* and having ascertained her berth go out and bring back a hundred men to take her.

Not finding the object of our search at the anchorage inside either bar or at the quarantine, I continued on up the river. The moon was shining brightly on our side as we came up abreast of fort Anderson and suddenly the

---

[28]*stem*, curved timber that extends from keel to bowsprit, sealing and protecting a wooden ship's bow. The *stem* is usually made of several laminated layers, the *false stem* being the outermost. The use of the word *false* in the term is obscure.

sentry's hail came across the water—"Boat ahoy!" The cry was repeated by a dozen voices and followed by the fire of musketry. It was too near daylight to make my way out, if I desired it, (and I did not) so I determined upon a bit of strategy.

Instantly turning the boat I let them see her in the moonlight apparently pulling rapidly down stream, then giving her a sheer with the helm I cut off the moon's rays from their line of sight, and my boat was invisible in the swell. In this manner I gained the shadow of the opposite bank and under its cover, pulled straight up towards Wilmington; leaving them to send their boats and alarm *down* the river.

Thus I passed safely by fort and obstructions, continuing on until within four miles of the City, when, as it was daylight I prepared for concealment.

We landed and hauled the boat, by great effort, over a strip of sand into some swamp grass; concealing it with branches of trees; after which we stowed ourselves away in the bushes on the bank, close to the channel and in a fine position to see all movements of vessel[s] in the river. Eight steamers passed us during the day—amongst them the *Yadkin* flagship of the rebel Commodore Lynch, but no iron clad appeared. Just at dark two boats came close in around a point of marsh and looked like an attacking party—so with my men all ready behind a log, I walked out and hailed them; ordering them to surrender. This they did; but proved to be a fishing party of white men from Wilmington. From them I learned that the *Raleigh* had run upon a bar at high water and that as tide fell, the weight of armor had caused her to split open. She was under water. My next thought was to learn all that was possible about the batteries, roads and obstructions, as I knew that our government soon intended a movement on so important and troublesome a place. Taking the fishermen as guides we moved to the city, examining everything and discovered the nature of the channel obstructions. Pulling down again we went into a creek about four miles below the town and made our way through a cypress swamp to a road which we started off to explore. Finding the main turnpike and telegraph, two miles off, I hastened to station myself with eight men at the junction of it, with two other roads, leaving the rest of the men in ambush near our boat. We were just outside the rebel city in the midst of swarms of soldiers, and lines of fortifications, and it was policy to keep very quiet, but we were growing hungry and a little cross and did not long suffer people to pass unmolested. The first man captured was a hunter, who proved to be keeper of a store a mile away—the next was the army mail-carrier with a bag of four hundred letters and documents—which were eagerly overhauled—discovering the plan and strength of the defenses and number of men in rebel garrisons.

The next thing to be thought of was food. Those who fight must eat and our hard tack and salt horse[29] had long since disappeared. Mr. Howorth was therefore dressed in the hat and jacket of the Georgia cavalryman; mounted upon his horse and started off to the store of our captured friend, with a pocket full of confederate money taken from the mail, and the "brass" requisite for his dangerous adventure. I call it dangerous, not only because of the danger of detection but by reason of the necessity for wearing a rebel private's hat and coat,[30] which would usually be found alive after their owner was cold upon a battle field.

This gallant officer returned safely, after mingling freely with soldiers, and having to spin a long yarn to an inquisitive female who had a brother in the place which he named as his home. The chickens and milk that he brought back were excellent and had only been obtained by a free use of the storekeeper's name; whom he declared he had met, hunting down the road and who had expressly told him to say to Lizzy "that I tell her to sell 'em." These articles with the blackberries growing near us formed a meal that could not be improved in Seceshia,[31] and left us ready for anything. Although we permitted most people to pass unmolested, there were some whom it was policy to take, and in the afternoon I found my eight men guarding twenty-six prisoners, any one of whom with pluck enough to shout, might bring down upon us a swarm of "chivalry." This was becoming too much like the Irishman's tartan[32]—and I concluded only to wait for the courier from the city, for the evening papers and Richmond news, before making for the boat. Mounting a horse I posted myself like a highwayman by the road side and awaited his coming; but concluded in the mean time to send my prisoners under guard down to the swamp. This move was unfortunate for just as they filed across the road into the woods, my expected mail carrier came over a knoll, two hundred yards away, with another mounted man in company. Seeing the blue shirts and carbines they knew at once what had become of the morning courier and instantly wheeled about. I pursued but to no purpose, my "cavalry brigade"[33] was tired and soon distanced. I now for the first time, cut the wires to prevent them from sending a message to Fort Fisher, and

---

[29]salt beef.

[30]That is, the hat and coat were infested with lice and, hence, "alive."

[31]*Seceshia*, a term for the seceded states fairly common in the North, South, and abroad during the war years. Vaguely literary and romantic abroad and in the South, it tended to be used sarcastically in the North.

[32]No explanation found, but Cushing seems to be referring to an Irishman's kilt that was insufficiently long or protective. Possibly a reference to a joke.

[33]That is, his horse.

made for the boat with all speed—placed my prisoners in canoes, took them in tow and moved down towards the river, which we entered at dusk.

I now determined to place the most of the captured men in the light house on Marsh Island, which had no keeper—and then escape before the pursuit should become too hot to permit it—but just as I neared it, the steamer *Virginia* rounded the point and came right at us. I instantly ordered the men to jump overboard and shove the boats in close to the marsh grass; holding their heads below the gunwale; and threatened any prisoner who spoke with immediate death. In the dark our ruse succeeded—the steamer passed within ten feet of us and failed to discover their Yankee visitors.

I now took away the oars and sails from the canoes and set twenty men adrift in the tideway, knowing that they would be picked up in the morning, and also made fast a note to a buoy—reminding Col Jones of his boast that I would never enter the harbor again. We had now to get down by Fort Anderson, Fort Fisher, the forts on Leeks Island, and batteries Campbell and "the Mound," and it was quite certain that their boats would be ready to intercept us at the bar. Passing Anderson undiscovered, we captured a boat load of soldiers, and were informed that there was a guard boat out, containing seventy five musketeers, waiting for us. The tide was now in our favor and I concluded to pull boldly for the bar—run foul of the guard boat—use cutlasses and revolvers and drift by the batteries in that way, since they would not fire on their own men. It was within an hour of daylight and everything was as bright in the moons rays as if dawn were indeed come. As we neared confederate point a boat was seen rising and falling with the swell, and our course was at once shaped for it. My men were eager to commence so unequal a fight, feeling confidence in themselves, in an encounter with five times their number of soldiers in the water. My orders were to wait for my word, and *then* all but the two bow oars "trail" and take to their arms while I sheered in and laid our boat aboard. The eight rebel soldiers with us I promised immediate death upon the least sign that they would aid their comrades.

When some fifteen yards from the object of attack, I ordered those not pulling to aim, and was about to pour in a broadside, when four more boats shot from Confederate Point, and five from Leeks Island; pulling so as to form a line across the whole entrance. At the first glimpse I saw the trap and formed the only plan that hope left me. With helm hard aport we went short around but only to find a large boat to windward, under canvass. We were now at the junction of the two channels, where the tide splits—one leading down seven miles below to [Fort] Caswell—where I had entered, and the other where I proposed to go out. At the Caswell entrance a south west gale had been blowing, and it was no doubt breaking clear across the bar, besides it would be daylight ere we could have passed Smithville or the forts, so our only chance was at Fisher. Dashing off with the tide in the direction of Smithville I passed the sail boat, and by my trick of sheering the cutter so as to avoid reflecting the moon's rays, caused the enemy's main line of boats to lose sight of her in the swell.

Being soldiers, they did not take into consideration the facts regarding the impossibility of escape at the west bar: and concluded that I was making for it. The whole line came after, in pursuit, leaving their original station unguarded. That was my time and it was improved. Suddenly turning we approached the sail boat as if to board, when her crew lost their nerve and tried to back. Missing stays,[34] they drifted off with the tide, while we shot around the semi-circle and cut under the stem of the line of boats in chase. Then they saw us—but too late. We gained the channel a hundred yards the start of the leading boat, and to prevent being blown out of [the] water by the forts, plunged boldly into the breakers upon Caroline Shoal and went through safely; the army boats not daring to follow. In this expedition I did not sleep for sixty-eight hours.

For this as for my previous visit to the harbor I received the official thanks of the Navy Department.

CSS *Albemarle*

About this time the government was laboring under the anxiety in regard to the condition of affairs in the Sounds of North Carolina. Some months previous,[35] a rebel iron-clad had made her appearance—attacking Plymouth, beating our fleet, sinking the *Southfield* and killing Capt Flusser who commanded the flotilla. Gen Wessels' brigade was forced to surrender, and all that section of country and line of [the] Roanoke River fell into rebel hands.

Little Washington and the Tar River were thus outflanked and lost to us. Some time after,[36] this iron-clad, the *Albemarle*, steamed out into the open sound and engaged nine of our steamers, doing much damage and suffering little. The *Sassacus* attempted to run her down, but failed, and had her boiler exploded by one of the 200-pdr shells fired from the confederate. The government had no iron clad that could cross Hatteras bar and enter the sounds; and it seemed likely that our wooden ships would be defeated; leaving Newbern [New Bern], Roanoke Island and other points endangered. At all events

---

[34]*missing stays.* The lubberly crew of soldiers mishandled the sails, and the boat—instead of falling onto a new tack—was caught in the eye of the wind and lost headway.

[35]April 19, 1864.

[36]May 5, 1864.

With her ram lodged in the Southfield's *starboard bow, the* Albemarle *was nearly pulled under before the Federal ship settled on the bottom.*
Battles and Leaders of the Civil War, The Century Co.: New York, 1884, Volume 4, p. 628.

it was impossible for any number of our vessels to injure her at Plymouth, and the expense of our squadron kept to watch her was very great. At this stage of affairs, Admiral S. P. Lee was speaking to me of the case and I proposed a plan for her capture or destruction. I submitted, in writing; two plans, either of which I was willing to undertake.

The first was based upon the fact that through a thick swamp the iron clad might be approached to within a few hundred yards. India rubber boats to be inflated and carried upon men's backs might be procured and transported by a boarding party of a hundred men, or two low pressure, and very small steamers, each armed with a torpedo and howitzer might constitute the offensive force. In this last named plan (which had my preference) I intended that one boat should dash in, while the other stood by to throw canister and renew the attempt, if the first failed. It would also be useful to pick up our men if the attacking boat were disabled. Admiral Lee believed that the plan was good, and ordered me to Washington to submit it to the Sec of Navy. Mr Fox[37] doubted the merit of the affair but concluded to order me to New York to "purchase suitable vessels." Finding some boats building for picket duty, I selected two, and proceeded to fit them out. They were open launches,

---

[37]Assistant Secretary of the Navy Gustavus Fox generally handled operational matters and correspondence for Secretary of the Navy Gideon Welles, leaving the latter free to handle political matters. See appendix 2 for a description of their superb working arrangement.

During the furious battle in Albemarle Sound on May 5, 1864, the Federal gunboat Sassacus rammed the Albemarle at top speed but inflicted only minor damage.

Battles and Leaders of the Civil War, The Century Co.: New York, 1884, Volume 4, p. 638.

about thirty feet in length, with small engines and propelled by a screw.[38] A twelve pounder howitzer was fitted to the bows of each, and a boom rigger out, some fourteen feet in length; swinging by a goose neck hinge to the bluff of the bow. A topping lift to a stanchion inboard; raised or lowered it, and the torpedo was fitted into an iron slide at the end. This was intended to be detached from the boom by means of a heel-jigger leading in board; and exploded by another line connecting with a pin which held a grape shot over nipple and cap.

The torpedo was, I believe, the invention of Engineer Lay of the navy and introduced by Chief Engineer Wood. It has many defects and I would not again attempt its use. Everything being complete we started to the south-ard—taking the boats through the canals to Chesapeake Bay, and losing one in going down to Norfolk. This was a great misfortune and I have never understood how so stupid a thing occurred. I forget the name of the volunteer Ensign to whose care it was entrusted, but am pleased to know that he was taken prisoner. I trust that his bed was not of down, or his food that of princes while in rebel hands.

My best boat being thus lost, I proceeded with one alone to make my way through the Chesapeake and Albemarle Canal into the Sounds. Half way through the canal was filled up, but finding a small creek that empties into it below the obstruction I endeavored to feel my way through. Encountering a mill dam, we waited for high water and ran the launch over it—below she grounded but I got a flat boat and taking out gun and coal succeeded, in two days, in getting her through.

Passing with but seven men through the canal, where for thirty miles there was no guard or union inhabitant I reached the Sound, and ran before a gale of wind to Roanoke Island. Here I pretended that we were going to Beaufort and engaged to take two passengers along. This deception became necessary in consequence of the close proximity of the rebel forces. If any person had known our destination the news would have reached Plymouth long before we arrived to confirm it.

So in the middle of the night I steamed off into the darkness, and in the morning was out of sight.

Fifty miles up the sound I found the fleet anchored off the mouth of the River and awaiting the Ram's appearance. Here I for the first time disclosed to my officers and men our object and told them that they were at liberty to go or not as they pleased. These seven in number, all volunteered. One

---

[38]A splendid reproduction of one of Cushing's launches has been built by Brush Creek Yachts of Plymouth, North Carolina, for the Port of Plymouth Museum.

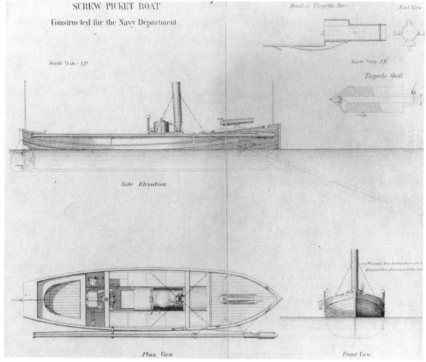

A screw launch with a spar torpedo slung on its starboard side. Cushing used a similar launch to sink the Albemarle.

"Screw Picket Boat, Constructed for the Navy Department," General arrangement plan published in *Submarine Warfare, Offensive and Defensive*, by Lieutenant Commander J. S. Barnes, USN, 1869. Naval History and Heritage Command.

of them [was] Mr Howorth of the *Monticello* who had been with me repeatedly in expeditions of peril. The names of all who went with me I give in conclusion. Six were added to my original force. Amongst these was Asst Paymaster Frank Swan; who came to me as we were about to start and urged that he might go, as he had never been in a fight. Disregarding my remark that "it was a bad time for initiation" he still made the request and joined us. He found an eventful night of it; being wounded and spending his next four months in Libby Prison and Salisbury.[39]

[39]Libby Prison in Richmond was reserved for Union officers. Because of its proximity to Washington, numerous escape attempts, and the number of prison narratives by its educated population, it is probably the best-known Civil War prison after Andersonville. Salisbury Prison in North Carolina was one of the first prisoner of war camps. Designed for a population of 2,000, it eventually housed more than 10,000, with predictable results. An estimated 11,700 Union soldiers were buried in eighteen trenches outside the prison walls. General George Stoneman burned the buildings on April 12–13, 1865, two weeks before General Joseph Johnston surrendered to General William T. Sherman, bringing the war's last campaign to a close. The site is now the Salisbury National Cemetery.

The Roanoke River is a stream averaging one hundred and fifty yards in width, and quite deep. Eight miles from the mouth was the town of Plymouth; where the ram was moored. Several thousand soldiers occupied town and forts, and held both banks of the stream.

A mile below the ram was the wreck of the *Southfield* with hurricane deck above water and on this a guard was stationed to give notice of anything suspicious or fire rockets in case of attack. Thus it seemed impossible to surprise them or to attack with hope of success. Impossibilities are for the timid—we determined to overcome all obstacles. On the night of the 27th of October we entered the river, taking in tow a small cutter with a few men; the duty of which was to dash aboard the *Southfield* at the first hail, and prevent any rocket from being ignited.

Fortune was with our little boat and we actually passed within thirty feet of the pickets without discovery; and neared the wharf where the rebels lay all unconscious. I now thought that it might be better to board and "take her alive"—having in the two boats twenty men, well armed with revolvers, cutlasses, and hand grenades. To be sure there were thousands near by, and ten times our number on the ship; but as surprise is everything and I thought that if her fasts[40] were cut, at the instant of boarding, we might overcome those on board, take her into the stream and use her iron sides to protect us after, from the forts. Knowing the town I concluded to land at the lower wharf, creep around, and suddenly dash aboard from the bank, but just as I was sheering in close to the wharf, a hail came sharp and quick from the iron clad—in an instant repeated. I at once directed the cutter to cast off, and go down to capture the guard left in our rear, and ordering all steam, went at the dark mountain of iron in front of us. A heavy fire was at once opened upon us not only from the ship but from men stationed on the shore: but this did not disable us, and we neared them rapidly. A large fire now blazed upon the bank, and by its light I discovered the unfortunate fact that there was a circle of logs around the *Albemarle* formed out from her side, with the very intention of preventing the action of torpedoes.

To examine them more closely I ran alongside until amidships; received their fire and sheered off for the purpose of turning, a hundred yards away and going at the booms squarely. This was my only chance of success; and even if my boat were forced over the obstruction, it could never get out again. But I was there to accomplish an important object, and to die, if needs be, was but a duty. As I turned, the whole back of my coat was torn out by buck shot and the sole of my shoe was carried away—the fire was very severe. In a lull of the firing the Captain hailed us; again demanding what boat it was. All

---

[40]*fasts*, mooring lines.

"The explosion took place at the same instant that one hundred pounds of grape at ten feet range crashed in our midst—and the dense mass of water thrown out by the torpedo came down with choking weight upon us."

Battles and Leaders of the Civil War, The Century Co.: New York, 1884, Volume 4, p. 638.

my men gave some comical answer, and mine was a dose of canister which I sent amongst them from the howitzer, buzzing and singing against the iron ribs and into the mass of men standing fire-lit upon the shore.

In another instant we had struck the logs and were over—with headway nearly gone—slowly forging up under the enemy's quarter port. Ten feet from us the muzzle of a rifle gun looked into our faces, and every word of command, on board, was distinctly heard.

Four more bullets now plunged through my clothing in quick succession as I stood in the bow; the heel jigger in right hand and exploding line left. We were near enough then; and I ordered the boom lowered until the forward motion of the launch carried the torpedo under the ram's overhang. A strong pull of the detaching line—a moment's waiting for the torpedo to rise under the hull, and I hauled in the left hand, just cut by a bullet. The explosion took place at the same instant that one hundred pounds of grape at ten feet range crashed in our midst—and the dense mass of water thrown out by the torpedo came down with choking weight upon us. Twice refusing to surrender, I commanded the men to save themselves, and throwing off sword, revolver, shoes and coat, struck out from my disabled and sinking boat into the river. It was cold—long after the frosts—and the water chilled the blood, while the whole surface of the stream was ploughed up by grape and musketry—and my nearest friend was twelve miles away—but anything was better than to fall into rebel hands.

Death was better than surrender. I swam for the opposite shore but as I neared it a man near me gave a great gurgling and went down.

The rebels were out on boats picking up my men and one of these attracted by the sound pulled in my direction. I heard my own name mentioned. I now struck out down the stream and was soon far enough away to again attempt landing. This time as I struggled to reach the bank I heard a groan in the river behind me, and although very much exhausted concluded to turn and give all the aid in my power to the officer or seaman who had bravely shared the danger with me and in whose peril I might in turn partake.

Swimming in the night with eye at the level of the water—one can have no idea of distance, and labor, as I did, under the discouraging thought that no headway is made. But if I were to drown that night, I had at least an opportunity of dying while struggling to aid another. Nearing the swimmer, he proved to be Act M. Mate Woodman, who said he could swim no longer. Knocking his cap from his head, I used my right arm to sustain him and ordered him to strike out.

For ten minutes at least, I think he managed to keep afloat when his presence of mind and physical force being completely gone, he gave a yell and sunk like a stone—fortunately not seizing upon me as he went down. Again alone upon the water, I directed my course towards the town side of the river, not making much headway, as my strokes were now very feeble.

My clothes being soaked and heavy, and little chop seas splashing with a choking persistence into my mouth every time that I gasped for breath. Still there was a determination *not* to sink: A will *not* to give up, and I kept up a sort of mechanical motion long after my bodily force was in fact expended.

At last, and not a moment too soon, I touched the soft mud; and in the excitement of the first shock, I half raised my body, and made one step forward; and then remained half in the mud and half in the water until daylight; unable even to crawl on hands and knees—with brain in a whirl and nearly frozen—but with one thing strong in me—the fixed determination to escape. The prospect of drowning, starvation, death in the swamps, all seemed lesser evils than that of surrender. As day dawned I found myself in a point of swamp that enters the suburbs of Plymouth, and not forty yards from one of the forts. The sun came bright and warm, proving a most cheering visitant, and giving me back a great portion of the strength of which I had been deprived before.

Its light showed me the town, swarming with soldiers and sailors, who moved about in an excited manner as if angry at some sudden shock. It was a source of satisfaction to me to know that I had pulled the wire that set all these figures moving, in a manner quite as interesting as the best of theatricals, but as I had no desire to be discovered by any of the dogs that were so plentiful around me, I did not long remain a spectator.

My first object was to get into a dry fringe of rushes that edge[d] the swamp; but to do this required me to pass over thirty or forty feet of open ground right under the eye of the sentinel who walked the parapet watching, until he turned for a moment, I made a dash to cross the space but was only half way over when he turned and forced me to drop down right between tow paths and almost entirely unshielded.

Perhaps I was unobserved because of the mud that covered me and made me blend in with the earth. At all events the soldier continued his tramp for some time while I, flat on my back, awaited another chance for action. Soon a party of four men came down the path at my right, two of them being officers and passed me so close as to almost tread upon my arm. They were conversing about the events of the previous night; and wondering how it was done, entirely unconscious of the presence of one who could give them the information. This proved to me the necessity of regaining the swamp—which I did by sinking my heels and elbows into the earth and forcing my body inch by inch towards it. For five hours then, with bare feet, head and hands, I made my way, where I venture to say none ever did before, until I came at last to a clear place where I might rest upon solid ground. The cypress swamp was a network of thorns and briers that cut into the flesh at every step like knives, and frequently when the soft mire would not bear my weight I was forced to throw my body upon it at length, and haul it along by the arms. Hands and feet were raw when I reached the clearing, and yet my difficulties were but commenced. A working party of soldiers was in the opening engaged in sinking some schooners in the river to restrict the channel. I passed twenty yards in their rear through a corn furrow, and gained some woods below. Here I encountered a negro and after serving out to him twenty dollars in greenbacks and some texts of scripture (two powerful arguments with an old darky) I had confidence enough in his fidelity to send him into town for news of the Ram. When he returned and there was no longer doubt that she had gone down I went on again plunged into a swamp so thick that I only had the sun for a guide and could not see ten feet in advance. About two in the afternoon I came out from the dense mass of reeds upon the bank of one of the deep narrow streams that abound there, and right opposite to the only road in that vicinity.

It seemed Providential that I should come just there; for thirty yards above or below, and I never would have seen it and might have struggled on until worn out and starved, I found a never to be discovered grave. As it was, my fortune had led me to where a picket party of seven soldiers were posted, having a little flat bottomed, square ended skiff, toggled to the root of a cypress tree that squirmed like a snake into the inky water. Watching them until they went back a few yards to eat I crept into the stream and swam over, keeping the tree between myself and them and making for the skiff.

Gaining the bank I quietly cast loose the boat and floated behind it some thirty yards, around the first bend where I got in, and paddled away as only a man could, where liberty was at stake. Hour after hour I paddled; never ceasing for a moment, first on one side, then on the other, while sunshine passed into twilight and that was swallowed up in thick darkness, only relieved by the few faint star rays that penetrated the heavy swamp curtain on either side.

At last I reached the mouth of the Roanoke and found the open sound before me.

My frail boat would not have lived a moment in the ordinary sea there, but it chanced to be very calm leaving only a slight swell, which was, however, sufficient to influence my boat so that I was forced to paddle all upon one side to keep her on the intended course. After steering by a star for where I thought the fleet might be, for perhaps two hours, I at length discovered one of the vessels; and after a long time got within hail.

My "Ship Ahoy!" was given with the last of my strength, and I fell powerless, with a splash into the water in the bottom of my boat, and awaited results. I had paddled every minute for twelve successive hours; and for four my body had been asleep "with the exception of my two arms and brain."

The picket vessel *Valley City*—for it was she upon hearing the hail, at once slipped her cable and got underway; at the same time lowering boats and taking precaution against torpedoes. It was some time before they would pick me up; being convinced that I was a rebel conductor of an infernal machine, and that Lieut Cushing had died the night before.

At last I was on board; had imbibed a little brandy and water, and was on my way to the flag ship commanded by Commander McComb.

As soon as it became known that I had returned rockets were thrown up and all hands called to cheer ship—and when I announced my success, all the commanding officers were summoned on board to deliberate upon a plan of attack. In the morning I was again well in every way with the exception of hands and feet, and had the pleasure of exchanging shots with the batteries that I had inspected on the day previous.

Admiral David Dixon Porter posed with his staff aboard his flagship, U.S.S. Malvern, shortly before the assault on Fort Fisher. Cushing is at far left.
Library of Congress.

I was sent in the *Valley City* to report to Admiral Porter at Hampton Roads; and soon after Plymouth and the whole district of the *Albemarle*, deprived of the iron clad's protection, fell an easy prey to Capt. McComb and our fleet. I again received the congratulations of the Navy Department and the thanks of the Congress of the United States. I was promoted to the grade of Lieut. Commander. The testimonials that I received from Chambers of Commerce, Cities, Union League Clubs &c were numerous and gratifying. I was at this time twenty-one years of age, having had my first command at nineteen. The *Albemarle* was built like the famous *Merrimac[k]* and in her contests with our ships successfully resisted solid hundred powder Dahlgren and Parrott shot, at ten yards range. In November 1864 I assumed command of the Flag Ship *Malvern* bearing the broad pennant of Rear Admiral David D. Porter. A large fleet was collected in Hampton Roads and it was known that Wilmington was the point of attack.

Fort Fisher

A combined army and navy movement was made against Fort Fisher in December and resulted in a failure, in consequence of the generalship of Gen

B. F. Butler, who would not assault; after a bombardment from the ships that kept the weak and surprised garrison so effectually in their bomb proofs that their flag was taken openly down the beach in the broad sunlight.[41]

The indignation of army and navy at this inexcusable conduct of Butler's was openly and loudly expressed, and we all rejoiced when another attack was ordered, under a man who would not permit great egotism and a jealous temper to make him blind to his duty as a soldier.[42] In the first attack I took my gig and went in on the bar to sound and put down buoys. I was six hours upon this dangerous duty; and congratulate my self that we were not blown out of the water. Round shot, shell and shrapnel ploughed around us every moment, and I actually had to bail out the water that was thrown into the boat by them. A cutter assisting us was sunk by the severe fire.

There is no doubt that this was the most dangerous service rendered during the day. This was the scene of the famous Powder Boat explosion.[43] I was sounded in Washington, by Mr. Fox, as to my willingness to perform the service of firing the powder; and at once consented to do so, as I had, early in the war to the taking in of a powder ship to Sumter for the same purpose. But afterward Commander Rhind was placed in command of the expedition which failed from no fault of his.

The day after the withdrawal of the troops a volunteer Lieut, commanding an armed prize, came around from the western bar and reported that he had been chased away by a rebel privateer loaded down with men and protected by cotton bales. The Admiral at once sent for me and did me the honor to propose that I should capture her—giving me again command of my old favorite the *Monticello* for the purpose. Steaming around the shoal as rapidly as possible, I found the vessel described, at anchor inside the bar under the guns of Fort Caswell, and fired a blank cartridge as a challenge. This did not draw her out, nor did the subsequent destruction of a large blockade running steamer, which I drove ashore under the batteries, in her attempt to get in. In this service my ship was hulled six times. The *Chickamaugua* would not fight, probably suspecting

---

[41]Cushing's meaning is unclear. He may be referring to the shooting away of Fort Fisher's flag by the bombardment while the fort's occupants were too busy hiding to raise it again. (Frequently gun crews wasted many shots trying for the prestige of shooting away a fort's flag, their missed shots flying harmlessly over more meaningful targets.) Or Cushing may be asserting that the landing force was able to carry its flag across the beach in plain sight of the fort's guns because the bombardment had forced the fort's inhabitants to seek shelter.

[42]Brigadier General Alfred H. Terry. Like most professional officers in both army and navy, Cushing despised Terry's predecessor, Major General Benjamin Butler. Ironically, Terry was also an amateur, but one possessed of the gifts and temperament of a fine combat officer.

[43]Late in 1864, Major General Benjamin Butler pushed the idea that exploding a ship carrying a huge load of powder close to Fort Fisher would destroy the fort. The attempt was made on December 23, when the small steamer *Louisiana*, loaded with 215 tons of powder, was exploded near but not nearly close enough to Fort Fisher. The failure was widely viewed as a farce. For a fuller description of the attempt see the listing for Alexander Rhind in appendix 2.

some Yankee trap—whereas nothing was desired by us but a fair field and no favor. With her extra men aboard she was much the stronger and might better have finished her career in a gallant action on the ocean; than in the way she did—sunk by a retreating crew in Cape Fear River.

On the 12th of January everything being ready, the attack was resumed against the forts of Wilmington. These mounted nearly a hundred heavy guns, and warned by Butler's fiasco, were garrisoned by over three thousand veteran soldiers. The ships, sixty in number, advanced in beautiful or-der—the ironclads taking the lead and followed by the heavy frigates—after which in turn came sloops of war and gun boats. The fire from the fleet was terrific and soon drove the enemy into shelter. For three days the bombard-ment continued, in which time most of the opposing guns were disabled and the time came to assault. On the morning of the 15th the Admiral observing the *Chickamauga* and some other steamers maneuvering to reinforce the forts inside, ordered me to drive them away. In order to do this I ran my wooden vessel[44] inside of the iron clad line and all other ships—nearest to Fort Fisher; where I moved head and stern and opened fire upon the steamers with my 100-pdr parrott and with broadside guns upon the Fort. After driving those vessels from position; the fire was continued upon the embrasures.

About two in the afternoon I landed with forty men to join the assault-ing body of sailors and marines who were to storm the sea front of the fort. These were fourteen hundred in number; the officers all in uniform, bright with gold lace and every man dressed as for inspection. All were armed with cutlass and revolver alone, excepting the marines, who carried muskets and were to cover us in scaling the works.

Wheeling from column into line, we marched up by the flank to within four hundred yards of the frowning fort and lay down under the slope of sand beach until the signal for assault should come from the army—who were to advance from the other side.

Lieut Ben Porter and myself massed our men and agreed to lead the as-sault—bearing with us the Admiral's blue flag. In the meantime, while we waited, the whole fire of the navy passed a few feet over our heads. Such a hell of noise I never expect to hear again. Hundreds of shell were in the air at once, varying from the five hundred pounders of the ironclads to those of a half and fourth of that weight but all shrieking in a grand martial chorus that was a fit-ting accompaniment to the death dance of the hundreds about to fall. At last the signal came, and we were up in an instant, advancing steadily, until within a hundred yards, and then bursting forward with a cheer from the whole line.

---

[44]*wooden vessel, the Monticello.*

The beach to be gone over was level white sand, into which we sank ankle deep, and which in the bright sunlight made targets of us all from contrast. The rebels meanwhile were not idle, but thinking ours the main storming party, massed against us and sent a staggering fire into our ranks that ploughed through with deadly effect; and never ceased for an instant. We gained the palisades only to find further advance impossible and all were brought to a halt. Thinking that I saw an opening I sprang forward and had proceeded some distance when upon looking behind me I perceived that I was not followed; so I went down in the sand for shelter.

In a moment I heard the voice of one of my men crying "Capt Cushing! They are retreating sir!" and upon looking around I saw the whole line breaking and going backward. A hundred yards was now between myself and the retreating force; and I was close under the muzzles of the Confederate rifles; but I made up my mind that it was my duty to join my men and rally them—so I sprang to my feet amidst what can only be called a storm of bullets and passed unharmed to our force. That retreat was a fearful sight. The dead lay thickly strewn along the beach, and the wounded falling constantly, called for help to their comrades, and prayed to God that they might not be left behind. I saw the wounded stagger to their feet all weak and bloody, only

The fleet's landing force suffered a blood repulse at the sea face of Fort Fisher, distracting the Confederate defenders just long enough for Union soldiers to grab a foothold on the land face.
Library of Congress.

to receive other and more fatal wounds and fall to rise no more. Our attempt had the good result of diverting the rebels' attention from the army who surprised their rear, and gained a hold upon their traverses—a seizure that was gradually increased until all was in our possession. Noble Ben Porter had met his death early in our assault, as well as Lieut Preston—and many of the officers had remained under the palisades of the fort until it should be dark. Amongst these were most of the ranking officers, including fleet Captain Breese who commanded the attack. I therefore assumed command and after intense exertion and fatigue succeeded in collecting a few hundred men with whom I again proceeded to assault, when I was met by an aid of Gen Terry who requested me to place my men in the entrenchments in front of Gen Bragg's army that was about to attack us from the rear.

This I did, relieving a regiment which went in fresh to Gen Terry's assistance. At 10 that night the [fort's] entire rebel force surrendered. In the intermediate time, between the assault and the surrender, the tide had risen and drowned many of our wounded who fell upon the beach; and swept off into the remorseless ocean the hero clay of many a gallant sailor. How few realize at what a cost our Nation's unity has been *purchased*!

Wilmington

On the 16th I was ordered around to the West bar on a reconnaissance of the forts there. Anchoring my ship, I pulled in with five men and an officer in my gig, to demand the surrender of Fort Caswell. Finding it abandoned I hoisted the American flag and proceeded to take possession of several other batteries in the vicinity. Pushing on up to Smithville I received the surrender of the town from the Mayor and hoisted our flag on the fort, capturing there, large quantities of arms and provisions.

Rebel cavalry were in the streets but I took possession of a building at the end of the wharf, and loading a lot of muskets remained there with four men, while I sent away two sailors—with darky boats crews—on out to my ship for reinforcements, and the other up through the river to Fisher to notify the Admiral. That night I had two hundred sailors ashore and established myself as "Military Governor." Our first act was to seize the men who had piloted blockade runners over the bar. These I promised to hang, but finally concluded to spare them if they hoisted upon Oak Island the signal lights by which ships ran in and out.

My threat had its effect and the lights were stationed, while I prepared boats for boarding any such vessels as might be decoyed into our trap.

On the night of the 20th a large steamer came over the bar, and made the private signals to Fort Caswell. Of course these could not be answered; but my officer, as directed, hailed her, and said that all was right, that the signal corps was withdrawn to Smithville. Upon this, she came up and anchored.

When we boarded and informed the captain that his vessel was a prize, he was not the only one astonished. A champagne supper was in progress in honor of successfully running the blockade; at which several English army officers were making merry, confident that they were in the friendly and hospitable bosom of the Southern Confederacy.

As we sat down amongst them and ordered the steward to bring another case of champagne, their tongues were loosened and one in accents of English disgust, exclaimed—"Beastly luck!" "A most unmitigated sell!" responded number two.

Aye! gentlemen, and may you never meet better luck on the same errand! This was the steamer *Charlotte* loaded with arms and machinery, and reported one of the fastest in the trade. Ten minutes later the Confederate steamer *Stag* came in, loaded down with a valuable cargo and was captured in the same manner. But, while the plan and credit of success were all mine; it was not so with the prize money. The *Malvern* and several light vessels came down that very evening and being within signal distance were entitled to claim equal shares with us. But, one instance of absolute fraud, I must mention. The steamer *A. D. Vance* commanded by Lieut Commdr John Upshur, was anchored ten miles away, outside *the other bar* and could not have assisted the capture under any circumstances.

They did not know of the seizure of the prizes until the following noon, and yet claimed a share while all the other ships near her disclaimed to do so unfair a thing. Hiring a lawyer in New York, cunning and unscrupulous—and aided by a few false oaths from the volunteer officers and a false meaning letter from Capt Upshur; their claim was actually admitted in court with us. I handed, myself, to the District Judge a letter from Admiral Porter, who was present when the vessels were taken, denouncing the whole claim of the [A. D.] *Vance* as "a fraud; an act unworthy of officers of the Navy." If this was not theft I am unable to discern the difference.

On the night of the 5th of February, with fifty men, in three boats, I entered Little River; the same place where I previously stormed the battery—and proceeded with muffled oars to the small town of All Saints Parish, South Carolina. Landing in the fog and taking a negro for a guide I soon had all the houses under guard, without the knowledge of a single one of the inhabitants. Proceeding to a Confederate cotton store house, I seized the contents.

In the morning the good towns people were considerably astonished to find a blue jacket and musket at every door. As no one escaped we remained there quietly all day, enjoying the poultry and sweet potatoes that South Carolina nourished, and capturing such mails and soldiers as came along.

At night we drew off with our prizes without an attack from any of the bodies of soldiery in the immediate vicinity. Knowing that the news of our visit would draw forces from the inlets near by; we organized an expedition for the capture of a Confederate store house three miles back of Charlotte Inlet.

I now left the *Monticello* outside of Cape Fear River and went on board the Flag Ship *Malvern* near Fort Anderson which the navy was about to attack.

Here several nights in succession I went up close under the guns of the rebel fort, to examine the obstructions and torpedoes, and once pulled with my brother—Paymaster Cushing[45]—in company close up to the city. One night while I was on this duty I found a band of music playing in Anderson, and speeches being made by enthusiastic confederates, who were picturing in glowing terms the victories of the chivalrous South; and heaping whole continents of scorn upon the base and cowardly North.

The confederacy was about to tumble but they were blind to the fact. Their armies were all beaten, but one Southerner was still the sure conqueror of five yankees. It was bright moonlight and I enjoyed the music in which the bombast was sandwiched, exceedingly, but at length could not resist the temptation of sending a bullet amongst the crowd as a period to the speech making—at the same time consigning them, with a shout, to a place somewhat warmer than Dixie. I succeeded in astonishing them; but the way the grape shot flew around, for awhile, from their guns, was far from pleasant. Their discipline was evidently good. Every night that I went up after this, I carried on my observations to the music of rebel round shot; but night firing is very inaccurate and their ammunition was wasted.

In consequence of a formidable line of obstructions, and a quantity of torpedoes in front of this fort, it was decidedly unsafe to attempt running the fleet by its guns and until that *should* be done it had free communication with the city above. Our army was closing in upon its rear but could not command the river; and it became necessary for the Navy to act. I therefore proposed to Admiral Porter the construction of a mock *Monitor* such as was used by him upon the Mississippi River—and at once proceeded to construct it out of an old flat boat and some canvass. When complete it was not possible to distinguish between it and the real one near by; at two hundred yards distance.

---

[45]Milton Cushing.

Raised, stripped of armor, and towed to Norfolk, Albemarle *briefly became a tourist attraction before the war's closing events distracted public attention. The worm-eaten hulk was sold for scrap in 1867.*
Naval History and Heritage Command.

The tide there runs at about five knots speed and it was to be the motive power. Weighing one end of my iron clad much heavier than the other so as to take it straight up with the tide, I towed her up to within two hundred yards of the opening of the obstructions and cast adrift.

Up the river with the flood tide, she went, apparently steaming in spite of everything passed successfully.

The consequence was that the commanding confederate, knowing that the army was closing in behind him, and thinking a *Monitor* in the river above—evacuated in such haste as to leave the fourteen heavy guns unspiked, and magazine intact.

We took possession the next morning. Confederate officers told me afterwards that this was the true reason for their retreat, and swore like pirates at the imposition.[46]

I was soon after ordered up to Norfolk to fit a torpedo upon my ship's bows, to encounter the anglo-rebel ironclads[47] expected from Europe but after making ready, found that I was to be disappointed by their non-appearance.

---

[46]Brigadier General Johnson Hagood evacuated Fort Anderson's garrison in the early morning hours of February 19, 1865. The Union column moving around the Confederate flank to get in rear of the fort probably had more influence on the decision to evacuate than Cushing's ersatz *Monitor*. Indeed, the possibility of such a ruse had been discussed by officers of the garrison some days before.

[47]The "anglo-rebel" Laird rams were no longer a threat at this time, having been confiscated by the British government. The French-built *Stonewall* was probably the vessel Cushing referred to. See appendix 1.

Just as the bottom of the rebellion fell out at Richmond, I was detached, and granted leave of absence—

Seeing the last of the war at the age of twenty two, and without having received any serious wound; even though my clothing . . .

[Cushing's journal ends here with the bottom third of the sixty-eighth ledger-sized page torn away. It is not known if more pages followed.]

Afterword

Late in February 1865, Admiral Porter detached Cushing with orders to proceed to Norfolk to have a spar torpedo rigged on the bow of the *Monticello*. The idea was for the *Monticello* to attack the CSS *Stonewall*, a seagoing ironclad built in France and known to be en route for American waters.

While the *Monticello* underwent the alteration at Norfolk, Cushing traveled to Washington to deliver dispatches. Secretary Welles took him to see the president, who congratulated Cushing on his recent achievements and laughed heartily at Cushing's story of the faux ironclad he'd deployed against Fort Anderson on the Cape Fear River.

In the aftermath of the fall of Wilmington, the threat of the *Stonewall*, never great to begin with, largely evaporated. (The *Stonewall* would not arrive until after the war was over and would be turned over to Spanish authorities in Havana in exchange for funds to repatriate the crew.) Admiral Porter shortly issued orders detaching Cushing from the *Monticello*. Although he would not officially receive the orders until June, he almost certainly learned of them while in Washington.

Cushing marked time in the nation's capital for the next several weeks. The navy's job was all but done, and the war on land was rapidly drawing to a close as Grant tightened his grasp on Petersburg and Sherman drove north through the Carolinas. A year or two before, Cushing might have found an excuse to attach himself to the Army of the Potomac for the final act of the great drama, but he was physically exhausted. He sought leave to go home to Fredonia.

Cushing had never enjoyed a hearty constitution. He was subject to severe colds and grinding headaches. Willpower and ambition had fueled his ferocious energy, not great physical strength. Even in ordinary times, sea duty is physically taxing, but Cushing had gone out of his way in search of the most dangerous and strenuous assignments. Since the night he'd spent hours in the cold river after sinking the *Albemarle*, he'd been troubled by bouts of pain in his back. He needed rest and recuperation.

News of the fall of Richmond and the retreat of Lee westward reached Fredonia on April 3. That night a band and a parade of happy citizens marched to the Cushing house to serenade the local hero. Cushing delivered a brief, gracious thanks and then called for three cheers for the flag. He joined the throng for a night of celebration in the ballroom of the town's best hotel. A week later, news of Appomattox brought another celebration. Will spoke again, and again thanked the citizens for their accolades. But he excused himself early from the party and spent the rest of the night walking with his memories and his uncertain plans for the future.

At twenty-two, Cushing was a national hero and the youngest lieutenant commander in the history of the navy. Prize money had made him modestly wealthy.[1] Many companies would offer him undemanding positions and good salaries for the benefit of listing his name among their officers. But Will Cushing wanted only to continue in his beloved profession. The action he had always craved would inevitably become a rarity in a peacetime navy. Ahead lay years of tedious cruises on foreign stations, enervating stretches of routine shore duty, and periods of total inaction waiting for orders in a navy with too many quality officers for too few good berths. On his long walk, he may have considered resigning his commission or asking for an extended leave to command a merchant vessel. He may have pondered seeking service in the navy of another country as John Paul Jones had after the Revolution. He might even have considered going filibustering in the Caribbean. But Cushing was very much the patriot, and it seems unlikely that he entertained any of these possibilities for long. He loved the navy, and in the navy he planned to stay.

In mid-May 1865, Cushing was ordered to the New York Navy Yard. His orders were soon changed, and he was sent to the West Coast to become executive officer of the screw sloop USS *Lancaster*, flagship of the Pacific Squadron since 1859. In March 1866, Cushing was feted in San Francisco as "Albemarle Cushing." When *Lancaster* returned to the East Coast in March

---

[1]Cushing had been disappointed with the prize money from the sinking of the *Albemarle*, only about $18,000. Congress would later reopen the case, readjusting the claim to reflect the federal property regained with the recapture of Plymouth. In 1873, Cushing was awarded another $38,000.

1867, Cushing was detached and spent the next seven months awaiting orders. During his time in Fredonia, he courted Katherine Marie Forbes, a friend of his sister Isabel.

In October, he was given command of the gunboat USS *Maumee*, a 593-ton screw sloop of the *Kansas* class, then refitting at the Washington Navy Yard. He and Katherine agreed to wait until he returned from a cruise to the Far East before marrying. On the last day of the month, the squadron set sail.

Peacetime service had not diminished Cushing's aggressiveness, nor thickened his thin skin. In Rio de Janeiro he reacted violently to a perceived slight by a Brazilian naval officer. Commodore Melancthon Wooley ordered the *Maumee* to sea at once, muttering darkly to an aide: "If that young man stays here, he will bring on an international war."

Maumee sailed east around the Cape of Good Hope, calling at Cape Town, crossed the Indian Ocean to Batavia on the island of Java, called at Singapore, and reached Hong Kong, homeport of the Asiatic Squadron, on May 1, 1868. Admiral Stephen C. Rowan put Cushing and the *Maumee* to work chasing pirates in the South China Sea. Cushing took to the work with gusto, eventually sending so many suspect vessels to Hong Kong that he was told to ease up before he totally disrupted the coastal trade. In November, the *Maumee* called at Yokohama. Cushing had been feted widely during the *Maumee*'s voyage and was delighted to find that his fame as "Albemarle Cushing" was even known in Japan. In Edo Bay, he at last laid eyes on the *Stonewall*, now the Japanese cruiser *Kotetsu*, and graciously filled a request for supplies and engine parts from her captain.

Maumee continued patrolling for pirates and showing the flag for another year. In November 1869, Cushing and his crew were detached at Hong Kong. The *Maumee* was sold at auction to spare the expense of a return voyage. According to *Lincoln's Commando*, it was during the voyage home that Cushing wrote his memoir of Civil War service.

Back home, Cushing married Kate Forbes on February 22, 1870, in a ceremony the *Fredonia Censor* described in breathless terms. But while the young couple enjoyed their honeymoon, the editor of the *Journal* in nearby Jamestown wrote a vituperative piece that called Cushing "the most ineffable, idiotic young snob that ever trod leather." To make matters worse, the editor announced that Cushing had "blundered into notoriety [through an] act of insubordination."

Exactly what motivated editor Bishop's attack is hard to guess. He no doubt sold more papers, but he also took his life in his hands baiting such a sensitive and explosive man as Cushing. As anyone who truly knew Will Cushing

Lieutenant Commander William B. Cushing about 1870.
Courtesy of Rear Admiral T. T. Craven, USN, 1935. Naval History and
Heritage Command.

would have predicted, Cushing took action immediately on returning from his honeymoon. Accompanied by his father-in-law, Brigadier General David S. Forbes, he marched into Bishop's office. There, while Forbes barred the door, Cushing thrashed the editor with a rawhide whip. Employees of the paper eventually intervened, ejecting Cushing and Forbes from the building. That evening a sheriff's officer delivered warrants to the hotel where the two were staying. He was followed shortly after by a band and a crowd of citizens rallying to Cushing's support. With public opinion against him, editor Bishop didn't press charges, although he did issue another article, claiming that he had bested Cushing in the encounter. Cushing might have taken this as another occasion to employ his horsewhip, but he'd just received orders to ordnance duty in Boston and departed the scene without further disciplining the press.

Shore duty bored Cushing, but he was happy with the company of his new bride. In the spring of 1871, with Kate expecting, the Cushings bought a house in Medford, outside Boston. Cushing pronounced himself quite satisfied with the prospect of a family and a quieter life. But in May he received news that his brother Howard, a lieutenant in the cavalry, had been killed fighting Apaches. Four years Will's senior, Howard had served quietly in the quartermaster department during the war. Perhaps envious of the fame won by Alonzo and Will, he transferred to the cavalry after Appomattox. The news of Howard's death sparked some of the rashness in the Will Cushing who had nearly resigned his navy commission to command Alonzo's battery after the latter's death at Gettysburg. He announced that he would go to the Southwest to avenge Howard's death with or without the navy's permission. Kate reasoned him out of the plan with the reminder that he would soon be a father. Still, the grief and strain of Howard's death devastated his health. He came down with pneumonia and suffered a recurrence of the back and hip pain that had troubled him for years. He was ill most of the summer, sitting for hours unable to summon the energy to do more than stare at pictures of his dead father and siblings. Of the eleven Cushing children, only Will, his brother Milton, and his sister Isabel still lived. Will himself was not yet twenty-nine, but he felt and looked much older, thoughts of his own mortality weighing on him with a heaviness that the Will Cushing of *Albemarle* days would have scorned.

His health improved late in the summer, and he returned to full duty over his wife's objections that he was not yet ready. He suffered a relapse in November, but his health and mood improved when Kate delivered a daughter, Marie Louise, on December 1. In January 1872, Cushing was promoted to commander. The following month he was detached to await orders. He had grown terribly thin after the months of illness, and his seniors urged him to seek rest in a better climate until he recovered. Will, Kate, and Marie departed for Washington. In the succeeding months, Cushing sought the advice of specialists, but the state of medical science had not advanced to the point anyone could determine the actual cause of his back and hip misery. Told Cushing's symptoms, doctors of a later generation would theorize that he was suffering from prostate cancer, tuberculosis of the hip, or a ruptured disk.

Despite his superiors' counsel that he should try a tropical clime, the Navy Department was slow to respond to his request for orders to Pensacola. In the spring of 1872, Cushing took his wife and daughter to the family home in Fredonia for the summer. They expected to go to Pensacola when cooler weather came, but Cushing's health broke down again in the fall, forcing the cancellation of his orders. Finally, in June of 1873, after more than a year in Fredonia, he received orders to command of the sloop of war *Wyoming*, bound for the Caribbean station. Kate, pregnant again, was not enthusiastic, but the prospect of a choice command rejuvenated Cushing. He departed Fredonia for Hampton Roads in late June to go to sea again.

Cushing was delighted with the *Wyoming*, one of the navy's most modern and powerful ships. (Her sister ship, the *Kearsarge*, had fought and sunk the famed Confederate cruiser *Alabama*.) Just short of 200 feet long and displacing 1,457 tons, she had a high raked bow that allowed a respectable speed of eleven knots under steam. She carried six heavy guns, representing a shift in design from numerous broadside guns to a small number of heavier guns mounted on pivots. *Wyoming* had spent her entire Civil War service in the Pacific, most of it in the Far East protecting American trading interests and searching for Confederate raiders. Fully refitted at Norfolk after her arduous duty far from American shipyards, she was the command Cushing had dreamed of since he'd first felt the call of the sea as a boy.

The *Wyoming* set sail for the Caribbean in August, making port calls at Bermuda and Kingston, Jamaica, before setting course for Aspinwall on the Isthmus of Panama. Rebels had sparked one of the Isthmus's periodic civil wars, and the *Wyoming* was instructed to protect the eastern terminus of the American-built and -controlled railroad across the Isthmus. Cushing drilled his gun crews and prepared to dispatch landing parties ashore in case of trouble. In the second week in November he received urgent telegrams from the American vice consul at Santiago de Cuba. The filibustering ship *Virginius*, flying the American flag, had been captured by a Spanish gunboat off Jamaica and taken into Santiago. Since November 4, the military governor had tried and executed 53 of the 165 crew and passengers. Eight of the dead were United States citizens, and Vice Consul Schmitt feared that more would shortly face firing squads. Cushing raised anchor and steamed to the rescue.

Whether Cushing was exceeding his authority is a complicated question. His orders read that he was not to leave Aspinwall until relieved by another ship. But tradition awarded considerable discretion to the captains of warships on foreign stations and the high seas. The advent of the telegraph and underwater cables had curtailed that freedom considerably, but Cushing had never been much concerned with the niceties of the chain of command. Though older and more experienced than the young daredevil who had terrorized the North Carolina coast of the Confederacy, he was still "Albemarle Cushing," and the smell of action had the same effect on him as the scent of blood in the water had on a shark. He did stop briefly at Kingston to inspect the records of the recent port visit of the *Virginius*. Satisfied that she had the right to fly the American flag, he set course for Santiago.

Whether or not he was predisposed to this conclusion is another question. The *Virginius* was a notorious filibuster. A former Confederate blockade-runner, she had been purchased for the Cuban revolutionaries by supporters in the United States. She had been transporting military supplies and recruits for the revolution for three years, and her identity and questionable status were well known. Still, Cushing might well have argued that the lives of American citizens, no matter how engaged, were sufficient reason for strong action.

The *Wyoming* entered Santiago de Cuba cleared for action. The fear of an immediate confrontation eased as a pilot boat came alongside, as if *Wyoming* were any peaceful ship. Under Cushing's watchful eye, the pilot maneuvered the ship through the treacherous passage into the harbor. The *Wyoming* dropped anchor not far from the British man-of-war *Niobe*. Vice Consul Schmitt soon came aboard to report the situation. Captain Lambton Lorraine and the *Niobe* had been in port since November 7, but Lorraine's protests to the military governor, General Juan N. Burriel, had not stopped more executions on November 8, nor would Burriel promise that they would not resume.

Cushing was outraged both at the Spanish and the failure of Captain Lorraine to open fire when his protests were ignored. He dispatched a letter to the governor's palace denouncing the executions as "murder" and demanding an interview with Burriel. The general demurred, an act that Cushing perceived as a direct affront to the United States flag and to himself personally. Perhaps Burriel was as yet unaware of the sort of man who commanded the *Wyoming*. Certainly a wiser or better-informed general would have penned a more diplomatic response to such a proud and touchy man as Cushing, particularly when Cushing had six heavy guns ready to revenge an insult. Cushing responded with a letter abandoning any pretext of diplomatic nicety: "If I do not see General Burriel by the day after tomorrow, and if any more prisoners are executed, I shall open fire on the Governor's palace." He backed up the threat by clearing *Wyoming* for action, hanging chains over the sides to protect the boilers, and training his guns on the nearest Spanish warship.

Burriel needed no more convincing and immediately invited Cushing ashore. The interview took place on the pier. Burriel advanced, his hand outstretched, but Cushing kept his behind his back, demanding without preamble if any more prisoners would be shot. The general, obviously agitated, mumbled that he could not make such a promise without authorization from Havana. Cushing shot back: "In that case, sir, I must request that all the women and children be removed from the city. I would not harm them." The threat did its work, and Burriel caved in, agreeing not to execute more prisoners nor move them without orders from Havana.

Cushing visited the site of the executions, where he announced: "Spain will be driven from the West Indies. The shots which killed the passengers and crew of the *Virginius* have sounded the death knell of Spanish power in the Western Hemisphere."

Although gratified that Cushing had brought the executions to a halt, the Navy Department was horrified to hear that he was spouting such rhetoric. Secretary of the Navy George Robeson telegraphed Commander Daniel Braine, Cushing's old comrade-in-arms from Civil War days: "For God's sake hurry on to Santiago de Cuba. We are afraid that Cushing will do something."

Braine set sail at once from New York aboard the *Juniata*, arriving at Santiago on November 26. Taking control of the situation, he quickly reached an agreement for the release of the *Virginius* and the surviving crew and passengers to, ironically, the ineffectual Captain Lorraine of the *Niobe*. The *Virginius* was found barely seaworthy, and the survivors were taken to New York aboard the *Juniata*. The *Virginius* foundered off Cape Hatteras while under tow to New York.

A poorly informed press reported that Lorraine had been responsible for halting the executions. Few credited or even mentioned Cushing's leading role in the intervention. Although Congress and the Navy Department would review and approve Cushing's actions, he would never receive the credit due him from the public. The injustice would endure to the present in most accounts of the affair.

The *Wyoming* participated in squadron exercises for the rest of the winter, but her engines were proving balky despite her recent refit. In April, she was ordered to Norfolk for repairs. Cushing was detached on April 24, 1874, and put on leave while awaiting reassignment. By then it was obvious that he was extremely ill. Cushing had both supporters and detractors aplenty in the navy, but even the least kindly disposed were shocked at the appearance of the once dashing young officer. He had become gaunt and walked with a limp. He was curt and touchy, his gray eyes glaring from deep sockets of pain and fatigue.

Cushing arrived in Fredonia in early May. His wife was horrified by his appearance, later telling his mother that Will looked more like a man of sixty than thirty-one. His habitual energy had lost its optimism and taken on a desperate quality. Within days, he left Kate, Marie Louise, and his new daughter, Katherine Abell, to prepare a home for his family convenient to his new duties as executive officer of the Washington Navy Yard. The Navy Department intended this as a light assignment where Cushing could rest and recover his health. But the succeeding summer brought little improvement. On Thanksgiving Day, Will, Kate, and Will's mother went to church and then sightseeing. They drove home through a cold rain for Thanksgiving dinner. Cushing sat up all night in terrible pain. He was no better over the weekend, but insisted on going to work on Monday. He managed to last through the day but arrived home in such agony that he immediately took to his bed.

It would prove his deathbed. The hero of the sinking of the *Albemarle* would linger in terrible pain for another three weeks. Morphine injections only dulled the pain, and he was delirious much of the time, recognizing neither Kate nor his mother. On December 8, Kate could no longer care for him at home, and he was transferred to the nearest hospital, the Government Hospital for the Insane. (Some of his enemies would subsequently spread the canard that he had gone insane as validation for their accusation that he had always been unstable.) In his final moments Cushing regained lucidity. On December 17, he awoke, called for Kate and embraced her and his mother. Together they recited the Lord's Prayer. Moments later he died peacefully, age thirty-two years, one month, and fourteen days.

Commander William Barker Cushing, USN, is buried at the United States Naval Academy at Annapolis, above his name a single word: *ALBEMARLE*.

ॐ

From Battles and Leaders of the Civil War

Being for the Most Part Contributions by Union and Confederate Officers

Based on "The Century War Series" published from November 1884 to November 1887 in *Century* magazine and edited by Robert Underwood Johnson and Clarence Clough Buel of the editorial staff of the *Century* magazine

New York: The Century Co., 1887–1888.

The First Battle of the Confederate Ram *Albemarle*

By Her Builder, Gilbert Elliott
In the spring of 1864 it was decided at Confederate headquarters that an attempt should be made to recapture Plymouth. General Hoke was placed in command of the land forces, and Captain J. W. Cooke received orders to cooperate with the *Albemarle*, an iron-clad then nearly finished. Accordingly Hoke's division proceeded to the vicinity of Plymouth and surrounded the town from the river above to the river below, and preparation was made to storm the forts and breastworks as soon as the *Albemarle* could clear the river front of the Federal war vessels protecting the place with their guns.

On the morning of April 18th, 1864, the *Albemarle* left the town of Hamilton and proceeded down the river toward Plymouth, going stern foremost, with chains dragging from the bow, the rapidity of the current making it impracticable to steer with her head down-stream. She came to anchor about three miles above Plymouth, and a mile or so above the battery on the bluff at Warren's Neck, near Thoroughfare Gap, where torpedoes, sunken vessels, piles, and other obstructions had been placed. An exploring expedition was sent out, under command of one of the lieutenants, which returned in about two hours, with the report that it was considered impossible to pass the obstructions. Thereupon the fires were banked, and the officers and crew not on duty retired to rest.

Having accompanied Captain Cooke as a volunteer aide, and feeling intensely dissatisfied with the apparent intention of lying at anchor all that night, and believing that it was "then or never" with the ram if she was to accomplish anything, and that it would be foolhardy to attempt the passage of the obstructions and batteries in the daytime, I requested permission to make a personal investigation. Captain Cooke cordially assenting, and Pilot John Luck and two of the few experienced seamen on board volunteering their services, we set forth in a small lifeboat, taking with us a long pole, and arriving at the obstructions proceeded to take soundings. To our great joy it was ten feet of water over and above the obstructions. This was due to the remarkable freshet then prevailing; the proverbial "oldest inhabitant" said, afterward, that such high water had never before been seen in Roanoke River. Pushing on down the stream to Plymouth, and taking advantage of the shadow of the trees on the north side of the river, opposite the town, we watched the Federal transports taking on board the women and children who were being sent away for safety, on account of the approaching bombardment. With muffled oars, and almost afraid to breathe, we made our way back up the river, hugging the northern bank, and reached the ram about 1 o'clock, reporting to Captain Cooke that it was practicable to pass the obstruction provided the boat was kept in the middle of the stream.

Captain Cooke instantly aroused his men, gave the order to get up steam, slipped the cables in his impatience to be off, and started down the river. The obstructions were soon reached and safely passed, under a fire from the fort at Warren's Neck which was not returned. Protected by the iron-clad shield, to those on board the noise made by the shot and shell as they struck the boat sounded no louder than pebbles thrown against an empty barrel. At Boyle's Mill, lower down, there was another fort upon which was mounted a very heavy gun. This was also safely passed, and we then discovered two steamers coming up the river. They proved to be the *Miami* and the *Southfield*.[1]

The two ships were lashed together with long spars, and with chains festooned between them. The plan of Captain Flusser, who commanded, was to run his vessels so as to get the *Albemarle* between the two, which would

---

[1]The *Miami* carried six nine-inch guns, one 100-pounder Parrott rifle, and one 24-pounder smooth-bore howitzer, and the ferryboat *Southfield* five nine-inch, one 100-pounder Parrott, and one 12-pounder howitzer.—Editors.

have placed the ram at a great disadvantage, if not altogether at his mercy; but Captain Cooke ran the ram close to the southern shore, and then suddenly turning toward the middle of the stream, and going with the current, the throttles, in obedience to his bell being wide open, he dashed the prow of the *Albemarle* into the side of the *Southfield*, making an opening large enough to carry her to the bottom in much less time than it takes to tell the story. Part of her crew went down with her.[2]

The chain-plates on the forward deck of the *Albemarle* became entangled in the frame of the sinking vessel, and her bow was carried down to such a depth that water poured into her port-holes in great volume, and she would soon have shared the fate of the *Southfield*, had not the latter vessel reached the bottom, and then, turning over on her side, released the ram, thus allowing her to come up on an even keel. The *Miami*, right alongside, had opened fire with her heavy guns, and so close were the vessels that a shell with a ten-second fuse, fired by Captain Flusser, after striking the *Albemarle* rebounded and exploded, killing the gallant man who pulled the lanyard, tearing him almost to pieces. Notwithstanding the death of Flusser, an attempt was made to board the ram, which was heroically resisted by as many of the crew as could be crowded on the top deck, who were supplied with loaded muskets passed up by their comrades below. The *Miami*, a very fast side-wheeler, succeeded in eluding the *Albemarle* without receiving a blow from her ram, and retired below Plymouth, into Albemarle Sound.

Captain Cooke having successfully carried out his part of the programme, General Hoke attacked the fortifications the next morning and carried them not, however, without heavy loss, Ransom's brigade alone leaving five hundred dead and wounded on the field, in their most heroic charge upon the breastworks protecting the eastern front of the town. General Wessells, commanding the Federal forces, made a gallant resistance, and surrendered only when further effort would have been worse than useless. During the attack the *Albemarle* held the river front, and all day long poured shot and shell into the resisting forts with her two guns.

The *Albemarle* and the *Sassacus*

By Edgar Holden, USN
On the 5th of May, 1864, the *Albemarle*, with the captured steamer *Bombshell*, and the steamer *Cotton Planter*, laden with troops, came down the Roa-

---

[2]Of the officers and men of the *Southfield*, seven of the former, including Acting Volunteer Lieutenant C. A. French, her commander, and forty-two of her men were rescued by the *Miami* and the other vessels of the Union fleet; the remainder were either drowned or captured.—Editors.

noke River. The double-enders *Mattabesett*, *Sassacus*, *Wyalusing*, and *Miami*, together with the smaller vessels, *Whitehead*, *Ceres*, and *Commodore Hull*, steamed up Albemarle Sound to give battle.[3]

The *Sassacus* was one of the several wooden side-wheel ships, known as "double-enders" built for speed, light draught, and ease of manoeuvre. She carried four 9-inch Dahlgren guns and two 100-pounder Parrott rifles, and was under the command of Lieutenant-Commander F. A. Roe.

The Union plan of attack was for the large vessels to pass as close as possible to the ram without endangering their wheels, deliver their fire, and then round to for a second discharge. The smaller vessels were to take charge of thirty armed launches, which were expected to accompany the iron-clad. The *Miami* carried a torpedo to be exploded under the enemy, and a strong net, or seine, to foul her propeller.

All eyes were fixed on this second *Merrimac* as, like a floating fortress, she came down the bay. A puff of smoke from her bow port opened the ball, followed quickly by another, the shells being aimed skillfully at the pivot-rifle of the leading ship, *Mattabesett*, cutting away rail and spars, and wounding six men at the gun. The enemy then headed straight for her, in imitation of the *Merrimac*, but by a skillful management of the helm the *Mattabesett* rounded her bow,[4] closely followed by our own ship, the *Sassacus*, which at close quarters gave her a broadside of solid 9-inch shot. The guns might as well have fired blank cartridges, for the shot skimmed off into the air, and even the 100-pound solid shot from the pivot-rifle glanced from the sloping roof into space with no apparent effect. The rapid firing from the different ships produced clouds of smoke. Changes of position were necessary to avoid being run down, and constant watchfulness to get a shot into the ports of the ram, as they quickly opened to deliver their well-directed fire. There was also danger of our ships firing into or entangling each other. As our own ship delivered her broadside, and fired the pivot-rifle with great rapidity at roof, and

---

[3]The Union force under Captain Melancton Smith in the action of May 5th, 1864, was: Double-enders: *Mattabesett*, Commander John C. Febiger; *Sassacus*, Lieutenant-Commander Francis A. Roe; *Wyalusing*, Lieutenant-Commander Walter W. Queen; *Miami*, Acting Volunteer Lieutenant Charles A. French. Ferry boat: *Commodore Hull*, Acting Master Francis Josselyn. Gun-boats: *Whitehead*, Acting Ensign G. W. Barrett; *Ceres*, Acting Master H. H. Foster. The losses were: *Mattabesett*, k, 2; w, 6,—total, 8; *Sassacus*, k, 1 ; w, 19 (13 of these were scalded)—total, 20; *Wyalusing*, k, 1,—in all 29.—Editors.

[4]If the *Mattabesett* rounded the bow of the *Albemarle*, the latter must have been heading up the sound at the time; in other words, she must have turned previous to the advance of the Union fleet. Upon this point the reports of the captains of the double-enders give conflicting testimony. Commander Febiger represents the ram as retreating toward the Roanoke, while Lieutenant Commander Roe describes her as in such a position that she would necessarily have been heading toward the advancing squadron. The conflict of opinion was doubtless due to the similarity in the two ends of the ram.—Editors.

port, and hull, and smoke-stack, trying to find a weak spot, the ram headed for us and narrowly passed our stern. She was foiled in this attempt, as we were under full headway; and swiftly rounding her with a hard-a-port helm, we delivered a broadside at her consort the *Bombshell*, each shot hulling her. We now headed for the latter ship, going within hail.

Thus far in the action our pivot-rifle astern had had but small chance to fire, and the captain of the gun, a broad-shouldered, brawny fellow, was now wrought up to a pitch of desperation at holding his giant gun in leash, and as we came up to the *Bombshell* he mounted the rail, and, naked to the waist, he brandished a huge boarding-pistol and shouted, "Haul down your flag and surrender, or we'll blow you out of the water!" The flag came down, and the *Bombshell* was ordered to drop out of action and anchor, which she did.

Now came the decisive moment, for by this action we had acquired a distance from the ram of about four hundred yards, and the latter, to evade the *Mattabesett*, had sheered off a little and lay broadside to us. The Union ships were now on both sides of the ram, with engines stopped. Commander Roe cried to the engineer, "Crowd waste and oil in the fires and back slowly! Give her all the steam she can carry!" To Acting Master Boutelle he said, "Lay her course for the junction of the casemate and the hull!" Then came four bells, and with full steam and open throttle the ship sprang forward like a living thing. It was a moment of intense strain and anxiety. The guns ceased firing, the smoke lifted from the ram, and we saw that every effort was being made to evade the shock. Straight as an arrow we shot forward to the designated spot. Then came the order "All hands lie down!" and with a crash that shook the ship like an earthquake, we struck full and square on the iron hull, careening it over and tearing away our own bows, ripping and straining our timbers at the waterline.

The enemy's lights were put out, and his men were hurled from their feet, and, as we learned afterward, it was thought for a moment that all was over with them. Our ship quivered for an instant, but held fast, and the swift plash of the paddles showed that the engines were uninjured. Through the starboard shutter, which had been partly jarred off by the concussion, I saw the port of the ram not ten feet away. It opened, and like a flash of lightning I saw the grim muzzle of a cannon, the gun's—crew naked to the waist and blackened with powder; then a blaze, a roar, and the rush of the shell as it crashed through, whirling me round and dashing me to the deck.

Both ships were under headway, and as the ram advanced, our shattered bows clinging to the iron casemate were twisted round, and a second shot from a Brooke gun almost touching our side crashed through, followed immediately by a cloud of steam and boiling water that filled the forward decks as our overcharged boilers, pierced by the shot, emptied their contents with a shrill scream that drowned for an instant the roar of the guns. The shouts of command and the cries of scalded, wounded, and blinded men mingled with the rattle of small-arms that told of a hand-to-hand conflict above. The ship surged heavily to port as the great weight of water in the boilers was expended, and over the cry, "The ship is sinking!" came the shout "All hands, repel boarders on starboard bow!" The men below wild with the boiling steam, sprang to the ladder with pistol and cutlass, and gained the bulwarks but men in the rigging with muskets and hand-grenades, and the well-directed fire from the crews of the guns, soon baffled the attempt of the Confederates to gain our decks. To send our crew on the grated top of the iron-clad would have been madness. The horrid tumult, always characteristic of battle, was intensified by the cries of agony from the scalded and frantic men. In the midst of all this, when every other man had left the engine-room, our chief engineer, Mr. Hobby, although badly scalded, stood with heroism at his post; nor did he leave it till after the action, when he was brought up, blinded and helpless, to the deck. An officer of the *Wyalusing* says that when the dense smoke and steam enveloped us they thought we had sunk, till the flash of our guns burst through the clouds followed by flash after flash in quick succession as our men recovered from the shock of the explosion,

To us, at least, there seemed time enough for the other ships to close in on the ram and sink her, or sink beside her, and it was thirteen minutes as timed by an officer of the *Wyalusing*; but the other ships were silent, and with stopped engines looked on as the clouds closed over us in the grim and final struggle.[5]

Captain French, of the *Miami*, who had bravely fought his ship at close quarters, and often at the ship's length, vainly tried to get bows on, to come to our assistance and use his torpedo; but his ship steered badly, and he was unable to reach us before we dropped away. In the meantime the *Wyalusing* signaled that she was sinking—a mistake, but one that affected materially the outcome of the battle. We struck exactly at the spot for which we had aimed; and, contrary to the diagram given in the naval report for that year, the headway of both ships twisted our bows, and brought us broadside to broadside—our bows at the enemy's stern and our starboard paddle-wheel on the forward starboard angle of his casemate.[6] At length we drifted off the ram, and our pivot-gun, which

---

[5]There was no lack of courage on the other ships, and the previous loss of the *Southfield*, the signal from the *Wyalusing* that she was sinking, the apparent loss of our ship, and the loss of the sounds of North Carolina if more were disabled, dictated the prudent course they adopted.—E.H.

[6]Against the report mentioned, I not only place my own observation, but I have in my possession the written statement of the navigator, Boutelle, now a member of Congress from Maine.—E.H.

Note: The Navy Department was not satisfied with the first official reports, and new and special reports were called for. As a result of investigation, promotions of many of the officers were made.—Editors.

had been fired incessantly by Ensign Mayer, almost muzzle to muzzle with the enemy's guns, was kept at work till we were out of range.

The official report says that the other ships then got in line and fired at the enemy, also attempting to lay the seine to foul his propeller—a task that proved, alas, as impracticable as that of injuring him by the fire of the guns. While we were alongside, and had drifted broadside to broadside, our 9-inch Dahlgren guns had been depressed till the shot would strike at right angles, and the solid iron would bound from the roof into the air like marbles. Fragments even of our 100-pound rifle-shots, at close range, came back on our own decks.

Commander Roe was asked to correct his report as to the speed of our ship. He had said we were going at a speed of ten knots, and the naval report says, "He was not disposed to make the original correction." I should think not!—when the speed could only be estimated by his own officers, and the navigator says clearly in his report eleven knots. We had, perhaps, the swiftest ship in the navy. We had backed slowly to increase the distance; with furious fires and a gagged engine working at the full stroke of the pistons—a run of over four hundred yards, with eager and excited men counting the revolutions of our paddles; who should give the more correct statement?

Another part of the official report states that the bows of the doubleenders were all frail, and had they been armed [armored] would have been insufficient to have sunk the ram. Our bow, however, was shod with a bronze beak, weighing fully three tons, well secured to prow and keel; and this was twisted and almost entirely torn away in the collision.

At dusk the ram steamed into the Roanoke River, never again to emerge for battle, and the object of her coming on the day of our engagement, viz., to aid the Confederates in an attack on New Berne, was defeated; but her ultimate destruction was reserved for the gallant Lieutenant Cushing, of glorious memory.

The Destruction of the *Albemarle*

By W. B. Cushing, Commander, USN

In September 1864, the Government was laboring under much anxiety in regard to the condition of affairs in the sounds of North Carolina. Some months previous (April 19th) a rebel iron-clad had made her appearance, attacking and recapturing Plymouth, beating our fleet, and sinking the *Southfield*. Some time after (May 5th), this iron-clad, the *Albemarle*, had steamed out into the open sound and engaged seven of our steamers, doing much damage and suffering little. The *Sassacus* had attempted to run her down, but had failed, and had had her boiler exploded. The Government had no iron-clad that could cross Hatteras bar and enter the sounds,[7] and it was impossible for any number of our vessels to injure the ram at Plymouth.

At this stage of affairs Admiral S. P. Lee[8] spoke to me of the case, when I proposed a plan for her capture or destruction. I submitted in writing two plans. The first was based upon the fact that through a thick swamp the ironclad might be approached to within a few hundred yards, whence India-rubber boats, to be inflated and carried upon men's backs, might transport a boarding-party of a hundred men; in the second plan the offensive force was to be conveyed in two very small low-pressure steamers, each armed with a torpedo and a howitzer. In the latter (which had my preference), I intended that one boat should dash in, while the other stood by to throw canister and renew the attempt if the first should fail. It would also be useful to pick up our men if the attacking boat were disabled. Admiral Lee believed that the plan was a good one, and ordered me to Washington to submit it to the Secretary of the Navy. Mr. Fox, Assistant Secretary of the Navy, doubted the merit of the project, but concluded to order me to New York to "purchase suitable vessels."

Finding some boats building for picket duty, I selected two, and proceeded to fit them out. They were open launches, about thirty feet in length,[9] with small engines, and propelled by a screw. A 12-pounder howitzer was fitted to the bow of each, and a boom was rigged out, some fourteen feet in length, swinging by a goose-neck hinge to the bluff of the bow. A topping lift, carried to a stanchion inboard, raised or lowered it, and the torpedo was fitted into an iron slide at the end. This was intended to be detached from the boom by means of a heel-jigger leading inboard, and to be exploded by another line, connecting with a pin, which held a grape shot over a nipple and cap. The torpedo was the invention of Engineer Lay of the navy, and was introduced by Chief-Engineer Wood. Everything being completed, we started to the southward, taking the boats through the canals to Chesapeake Bay. My best boat having been lost in going down to Norfolk, I proceeded with the other through the Chesapeake and Albemarle canal. Half-way through, the canal was filled up, but finding a small creek that emptied into it below the obstruction, I endeavored to feel my way through. Encountering a mill-dam,

---

[7]Several light-draught monitors were in course of construction at this time, but were not yet completed.—Editors.

[8]On September 5th, 1862, Acting Rear-Admiral S. P. Lee relieved Rear-Admiral Goldsborough of the command of the North Atlantic Squadron; he in turn was relieved by Rear-Admiral D. D. Porter, October 12th, 1864.—Editors.

[9]According to Engineer-in-Chief W. W. Wood, the launches were "45 to 47 feet long, 9 feet 6 inches beam. . . . Draught of water about 40 to 42 inches."—Editors.

we waited for high water, and ran the launch over it; below she grounded, but I got a flat-boat, and, taking out gun and coal, succeeded in two days in getting her through. Passing with but seven men through the canal, where for thirty miles there was no guard or Union inhabitant, I reached the sound, and ran before a gale of wind to Roanoke Island.

In the middle of the night I steamed off into the darkness, and in the morning was out of sight. Fifty miles up the sound I found the fleet anchored off the mouth of the river, and awaiting the ram's appearance. Here, for the first time, I disclosed to my officers and men our object, and told them that they were at liberty to go or not, as they pleased. These, seven in number, all volunteered. One of them, Mr. Howorth of the *Monticello*, had been with me repeatedly in expeditions of peril.[10]

The Roanoke River is a stream averaging 150 yards in width, and quite deep. Eight miles from the mouth was the town of Plymouth, where the ram was moored. Several thousand soldiers occupied town and forts, and held both banks of the stream. A mile below the ram was the wreck of the *Southfield*, with hurricane deck above water, and on this a guard was stationed. Thus it seemed impossible to surprise them, or to attack with hope of success.

Impossibilities are for the timid: we determined to overcome all obstacles. On the night of the 27th of October[11] we entered the river, taking in tow a small cutter with a few men, whose duty was to dash aboard the wreck of the *Southfield* at the first hail, and prevent a rocket from being ignited.

We passed within thirty feet of the pickets without discovery, and neared the vessel. I now thought that it might be better to board her, and "take her alive," having in the two boats twenty men well armed with revolvers, cutlasses, and hand-grenades. To be sure, there were ten times our number on the ship and thousands near by; but a surprise is everything, and I thought

---

[10]Cushing had already obtained a unique reputation in the service. His first notable exploit was a successful raid in November 1862, up New River Inlet, in North Carolina, in the tugboat *Ellis*. In January 1863, he captured by surprise an earth-work at Little River, his force consisting of 25 men in three cutters. In April he commanded the flotilla in the Lower Nansemond. Two important raids were made in Cape Fear River. The first was in February 1864. Its object was to capture General Hebért at Smithville. Taking two boats and twenty men, Cushing rowed past Fort Caswell in the darkness, landed at the town, and, concealing his men, took a small party with him to Hebért's headquarters. The general happened to be away, but one of his staff-officers was taken prisoner and carried to the boats. In June, Cushing took one cutter with fifteen men and went up nearly to Wilmington. Hiding his men during the day in a swamp, at night he embarked and made a reconnaissance of the obstructions below the city. At daybreak he landed again, and taking a party through the woods to the high road between Fort Fisher and Wilmington, he captured the courier with the mail from the fort. His third night was devoted to an examination of the Confederate gun-boat *Raleigh*, which was found to have been destroyed. On his way out he found a large force of guard-boats. His coolness and good judgment enabled him to elude them, and he returned without losing a man. On the strength of these exploits the Department entrusted him with the expedition against the *Albemarle*.—Editors.

[11]The first attempt was made on the previous night, but the launch grounded.—Editors.

if her fasts were cut at the instant of boarding, we might overcome those on board, take her into the stream, and use her iron sides to protect us afterward from the forts. Knowing the town, I concluded to land at the lower wharf, creep around, and suddenly dash aboard from the bank; but just as I was sheering in close to the wharf, a hail came, sharp and quick, from the iron-clad, and in an instant was repeated. I at once directed the cutter to cast off, and go down to capture the guard left in our rear, and, ordering all steam, went at the dark mountain of iron in front of us. A heavy fire was at once opened upon us, not only from the ship, but from men stationed on the shore. This did not disable us and we neared them rapidly. A large fire now blazed upon the bank, and by its light I discovered the unfortunate fact that there was a circle of logs around the *Albemarle*, boomed well out from her side, with the very intention of preventing the action of torpedoes. To examine them more closely, I ran alongside until amidships, received the enemy's fire, and sheered off for the purpose of turning, a hundred yards away, and going at the booms squarely, at right angles, trusting to their having been long enough in the water to have become slimy—in which case my boat, under full headway, would bump up against them and slip over into the pen with the ram. This was my only chance of success, and once over the obstruction my boat would never get out again. As I turned, the whole back of my coat was torn out by buckshot and the sole of my shoe was carried away. The fire was very severe.

In a lull of the firing, the captain hailed us, again demanding what boat it was. All my men gave comical answers, and mine was a dose of canister from the howitzer. In another instant we had struck the logs and were over, with headway nearly gone, slowly forging up under the enemy's quarter-port. Ten feet from us the muzzle of a rifle gun looked into our faces, and every word of command on board was distinctly heard.

My clothing was perforated with bullets as I stood in the bow, the heel-jigger in my right hand and the exploding-line in the left. We were near enough then, and I ordered the boom lowered until the forward motion of the launch carried the torpedo under the ram's overhang. A strong pull of the detaching-line, a moment's waiting for the torpedo to rise under the hull and, I hauled in the left hand, just cut by a bullet.[12]

---

[12]In considering the merits of Cushing's success with this exceedingly complicated instrument, it must be remembered that nothing short of the utmost care in preparation could keep its mechanism in working order; that in making ready to use it, it was necessary to keep the end of the spar elevated until the boat had surmounted the boom of logs, and to judge accurately the distance in order to stop the boat's headway at the right point; that the spar had then to be lowered with the same precision of judgment; that the detaching lanyard had then to be pulled firmly, but without a jerk; that, finally, the position of the torpedo under the knuckle of the ram had to be calculated to a nicety, and that by a very gentle strain on a line some twenty-five or thirty feet long the trigger-pin had to be withdrawn. When it is reflected that Cushing had attached to his person four separate lines, viz., the detaching lanyard, the trigger-line, and two lines to direct the movements of the boat, one of which was fastened to the wrist and the other to the ankle of the engineer; that he was also directing the

The explosion took place at the same instant that 100 pounds of grape, at 10 feet range, crashed among us, and the dense mass of water thrown out by the torpedo came down with choking weight upon us.

Twice refusing to surrender; I commanded the men to save themselves; and, throwing off sword, revolver, shoes, and coat, struck out from my disabled and sinking boat into the river. It was cold, long after the frosts, and the water chilled the blood, while the whole surface of the stream was plowed up by grape and musketry, and my nearest friends, the fleet, were twelve miles away; but anything was better than to fall into rebel hands, so I swam for the opposite shore. As I neared it a man [Samuel Higgins; fireman]; one of my crew, gave a great gurgling yell and went down.

The rebels were out in boats, picking up my men; and one of the boats, attracted by the sound, pulled in my direction. I heard my own name mentioned, but was not seen. I now "struck out" down the stream, and was soon far enough away again to attempt landing. This time, as I struggled to reach the bank, I heard a groan in the river behind me, and, although very much exhausted, concluded to turn and give all the aid in my power to the officer or seaman who had bravely shared the danger with me.

Swimming in the night, with eye at the level of the water, one can have no idea of distance, and labors, as I did, under the discouraging thought that no headway is made. But if I were to drown that night, I had at least an opportunity of dying while struggling to aid another. Nearing the swimmer, it proved to be Acting Master's Mate Woodman, who said that he could swim no longer. Knocking his cap from his head, I used my right arm to sustain him, and ordered him to strike out. For ten minutes at least, I think, he managed to keep afloat, when, his physical force being completely gone, he sank like a stone.

Again alone upon the water, I directed my course toward the town side of the river, not making much headway, as my strokes were now very feeble, my clothes being soaked and heavy, and little chop-seas splashing with choking persistence into my mouth every time I gasped for breath. Still, there was a determination not to sink, a will not to give up; and I kept up a sort of mechanical motion long after my bodily force was in fact expended.

At last, and not a moment too soon, I touched the soft mud, and in the excitement of the first shock I half raised my body and made one step forward; then fell, and remained half in the mud and half in the water until daylight,

---

adjustment of the spar by the halyard; that the management of all these lines, requiring as much exactness and delicacy of touch as a surgical operation, where a single error in their employment, even a pull too much or too little, would render the whole expedition abortive, was carried out directly in front of the muzzle of a 100-pounder rifle, under a fire of musketry so hot that several bullets passed through his clothing, and carried out with perfect success, it is safe to say that the naval history of the world affords no other example of such marvelous coolness and professional skill as were shown by Cushing in the destruction of the *Albemarle*.—J. R. Soley.

unable even to crawl on hands and knees, nearly frozen, with my brain in a whirl, but with one thing strong in me—the fixed determination to escape.

As day dawned I found myself in a point of swamp that enters the suburbs of Plymouth, and not forty yards from one of the forts. The sun came out bright and warm, proving a most cheering visitant, and giving me back a good portion of the strength of which I had been deprived before. Its light showed me the town swarming with soldiers and sailors, who moved about excitedly, as if angry at some sudden shock. It was a source of satisfaction to me to know that I had pulled the wire that set all these figures moving, but as I had no desire of being discovered my first object was to get into a dry fringe of rushes that edged the swamp; but to do this required me to pass over thirty or forty feet of open ground, right under the eye of a sentinel who walked the parapet.

Watching until he turned for a moment, I made a dash to cross the space, but was only half-way over when he again turned, and forced me to drop down right between two paths, and almost entirely unshielded. Perhaps I was unobserved because of the mud that covered me and made me blend with the earth; at all events the soldier continued his tramp for some time while I, flat on my back, lay awaiting another chance for action. Soon a party of four men came down the path at my right, two of them being officers, and passed so close to me as almost to tread upon my arm. They were conversing upon the events of the previous night, and were wondering "how it was done," entirely unaware of the presence of one who could give them the information. This proved to me the necessity of regaining the swamp, which I did by sinking my heels and elbows into the earth and forcing my body, inch by inch, toward it. For five hours then, with bare feet, head, and hands, I made my way where I venture to say none ever did before, until I came at last to a clear place, where I might rest upon solid ground. The cypress swamp was a network of thorns and briers that cut into the flesh at every step like knives; frequently, when the soft mire would not bear my weight, I was forced to throw my body upon it at length, and haul myself along by the arms. Hands and feet were raw when I reached the clearing, and yet my difficulties were but commenced. A working-party of soldiers was in the opening, engaged in sinking some schooners in the river to obstruct the channel. I passed twenty yards in their rear through a corn furrow, and gained some woods below. Here I encountered a negro, and after serving out to him twenty dollars in greenbacks and some texts of Scripture (two powerful arguments with an old darkey), I had confidence enough in his fidelity to send him into town for news of the ram.

When be returned, and there was no longer doubt that she had gone down, I went on again, and plunged into a swamp so thick that I had only the sun for a guide and could not see ten feet in advance. About 2 o'clock in the afternoon I came out from the dense mass of reeds upon the bank of one of the deep, narrow streams that abound there, and right opposite to the only road in the vicinity. It seemed providential, for, thirty yards above or below, I never should have seen the road, and might have struggled on until, worn out and starved, I should find a never-to-be-discovered grave. As it was, my fortune had led me to where a picket party of seven soldiers were posted, having a little flat-bottomed, square-ended skiff toggled to the root of a cypress-tree that squirmed like a snake in the inky water. Watching them until they went back a few yards to eat, I crept into the stream and swam over, keeping the big tree between myself and them, and making for the skiff. Gaining the bank, I quietly cast loose the boat and floated behind it some thirty yards around the first bend, where I got in and paddled away as only a man could whose liberty was at stake.

Hour after hour I paddled, never ceasing for a moment first on one side, then on the other, while sunshine passed into twilight and that was swallowed up in thick darkness only relieved by the few faint star rays that penetrated the heavy swamp curtain on either side. At last I reached the mouth of the Roanoke, and found the open sound before me. My frail boat could not have lived in the ordinary sea there, but it chanced to be very calm, leaving only a slight swell, which was, however, sufficient to influence my boat, so that I was forced to paddle all upon one side to keep her on the intended course.

After steering by a star for perhaps two hours for where I thought the fleet might be, I at length discovered one of the vessels, and after a long time got within hail. My "ship ahoy!" was given with the last of my strength, and I fell powerless, with a splash, into the water in the bottom of my boat, and awaited results. I had paddled every minute for ten successive hours, and for four my body had been "asleep," with the exception of my arms and brain. The picket-vessel, *Valley City*, upon hearing the hail, at once got under way, at the same time lowering boats and taking precaution against torpedoes. It was some time before they would pick me up, being convinced that I was the rebel conductor of an infernal machine, and that Lieutenant Cushing had died the night before. At last I was on board, had imbibed a little brandy and water, and was on my way to the flag-ship.

As soon as it became known that I had returned, rockets were thrown up and all hands were called to cheer ship; and when I announced success, all the commanding officers were summoned on board to deliberate upon a plan of attack. In the morning I was well again in every way, with the exception of hands and feet, and had the pleasure of exchanging shots with the batteries that I had inspected the day before. I was sent in the *Valley City* to report to

Admiral Porter at Hampton Roads, and soon after Plymouth and the whole district of the *Albemarle*, deprived of the iron-clad's protection, fell an easy prey to Commander Macomb and our fleet.[13]

Editor's Note

Lieutenant Cushing reached the *Valley City* about midnight on the night of October 28–29. On the next day, the 29th, at 11:15 A.M., Commander Macomb got under way, and his fleet proceeded up the Roanoke River. Upon the arrival of the fleet at the wreck of the *Southfield*, after exchanging shots with the lower batteries, it was found that the enemy had effectually obstructed the channel by sinking schooners alongside the wreck, and the expedition was therefore compelled to return.

On the next day, Commander Macomb, having ascertained from a reconnaissance by the *Valley City* that Middle River offered a clear passage, determined to approach Plymouth by that route. The expedition threaded the channel, shelling Plymouth across the woods on the intervening neck of land on its way up, until it reached the head of Middle River and passed into the Roanoke, where it lay all night.

At 9:30 on the morning of October 31, the line was formed, the *Commodore Hull* being placed in advance, as her ferryboat construction enabled her to fire ahead. The *Whitehead*, which had arrived with stores just before the attack, was lashed to the *Tacony*, and the tugs *Bazley* and *Belle* to the *Shamrock* and *Otsego*, to afford motive power in case of accident to the machinery. Signal was made to "Go ahead fast," and soon after 11 AM the fleet was hotly engaged with the batteries on shore, which were supported by musketry from rifle pits and houses. After a spirited action of an hour at short range, receiving and returning a sharp fire of shell, grape, and canister, the *Shamrock* planted a shell in the enemy's magazine, which blew up, whereupon the

---

[13]The list of officers and men on board *Picket-boat No. 1*, on the expedition of October 27, 1864, with the vessels to which they were officially attached was as follows: Lieutenant William B. Cushing, commanding, *Monticello*; Acting Assistant Paymaster Francis H. Swan, *Otsego*; Acting Ensign William L. Howorth, *Monticello*; Acting Master's Mate John Woodman, *Commodore Hull*; Acting Master's Mate Thomas S. Gay, *Otsego*; Acting Third Assistant Engineer William Stotesburg, *Picket-boat*; Acting Third Assistant Engineer Charles L. Steever, *Otsego*; Samuel Higgins, first-class fireman, *Picket-boat*; Richard Hamilton, coal-heaver, *Shamrock*; William Smith, ordinary seaman, *Chicopee*; Bernard Harley, ordinary seaman, *Chicopee*; Edward J. Houghton, ordinary seaman, *Chicopee*; Lorenzo Deming, landsman, *Picket-boat*; Henry Wilkes, landsman, *Picket-boat*; Robert H. King, landsman, *Picket-boat*. Cushing and Howorth, together with those designated as attached to the "*Picket-boat*," were the original seven who brought the boat down from New York. Cushing and Houghton escaped, Woodman and Higgins were drowned, and the remaining eleven were captured. For his exploit Lieutenant Cushing received the congratulations of the Navy Department and also the thanks of Congress and was promoted to the grade of lieutenant commander. The *Albemarle* was afterward raised, towed to Norfolk, and in 1867 there stripped and sold.—Editors.

Confederates hastily abandoned their works. In a short time Plymouth was entirely in possession of the Union forces. The casualties on the Union side were six killed and nine wounded.

The vessels engaged were as follows: double-enders: *Shamrock*, Commander W. H. Macomb, commanding division, Lieutenant Rufus K. Duer, executive officer; *Otsego*, Lieutenant-Commander H. N. T. Arnold; *Wyalusing*, Lieutenant-Commander Earl English; *Tacony*, Lieutenant-Commander W. T. Truxtun. Ferryboat: *Commodore Hull*, Acting Master Francis Josselyn. Gunboat: *Whitehead*, Acting Master G. W. Barrett. Tugs: *Belle*, Acting Master James G. Green; *Bazley*, Acting Master Mark D. Ames. The *Chicopee*, Commander A. D. Harrell, and *Valley City*, Acting Master J. A. J. Brooks, were not present at the second and final demonstration.—J. R. Soley.

Note on the Destruction of the *Albemarle*

By Her Captain, A. F. Warley, CSN

When I took command of the Confederate States iron-clad *Albemarle* I found her made fast to the river bank nearly abreast of the town of Plymouth. She was surrounded by a cordon of single cypress logs chained together, about ten feet from her side. There was no reason why the place might not be recaptured any day: the guns commanding the river were in no condition for use, and the troops in charge of them were worn down by ague, and were undrilled and worthless.

When I had been about a month at Plymouth the troops were relieved by a new set. On the day of their arrival I heard of a steam-launch having been seen in the river, and I informed the officer in command of the fact, and at the same time told him that the safety of the place depended on the *Albemarle*, and the safety of the *Albemarle* depended on the watchfulness of his pickets.

The crew of the *Albemarle* numbered but sixty, too small a force to allow me to keep an armed watch on deck at night and to do outside picketing besides. Moreover, to break the monotony of the life and keep down ague, I had always out an expedition of ten men, who were uniformly successful in doing a fair amount of damage to the enemy.

The officer in command of the troops was inclined to give me all assistance, and sent a picket of twenty-five men under a lieutenant; they were furnished with rockets and had a field-piece. This picket was stationed on board of a schooner about gun-shot below the *Albemarle*, where an attempt was being made to raise a vessel (the *Southfield*) sunk at the time of Commander Cooke's dash down the river. Yet on the night of the 27th of October Cushing's steam-launch ran alongside the schooner unobserved by the picket, without a sound or signal, and then steamed up to the *Albemarle*.

It was about 3 A.M. The night was dark and slightly rainy, and the launch was close to us when we hailed and the alarm was given—so close that the gun could not be depressed enough to reach her; so the crew were sent in the shield with muskets, and kept up a heavy fire on the launch as she slowly forced her way over the chain of logs and ranged by us within a few feet. As she reached the bow of the *Albemarle* I heard a report as of an unshotted gun, and a piece of wood fell at my feet. Calling the carpenter, I told him a torpedo had been exploded, and ordered him to examine and report to me, saying nothing to any one else. He soon reported "a hole in her bottom big enough to drive a wagon in." By this time I heard voices from the launch: "We surrender," etc., etc., etc. I stopped our fire and sent out Mr. Long, who brought back all those who had been in the launch except the gallant captain and three of her crew, all of whom took to the water. Having seen to their safety, I turned my attention to the *Albemarle* and found her resting on the bottom in eight feet of water, her upper works above water.

That is the way the *Albemarle* was destroyed, and a more gallant thing was not done during the war. After her destruction, failing to convince the officer in command of the troops that he could not hold the place, I did my best to help defend it. Half of my crew went down and obstructed the river by sinking the schooner at the wreck, and with the other half I had two 8-inch guns commanding the upper river put into serviceable order, relaid platforms, fished out tackles from the *Albemarle*, got a few shells, etc., and waited. I did not have to wait long. The fleet steamed up to the obstructions, fired a few shells over the town, steamed down again, and early next morning rounding the island were in the river and opened fire.

The two 8-inch guns worked by Mr. Long and Mr. Shelley did their duty, and I think did all that was done in the defense of Plymouth. The fire of the fleet was concentrated on us, and one at least of the steamers was so near that I could hear the orders given to elevate or depress the guns. When I felt that by hanging on I could only sacrifice my men and achieve nothing, I ordered our guns spiked and the men sent round to the road by a ravine. The crew left me by Captain Maffitt were good and true men, and stuck by me to the last.

The Defense of Fort Fisher

By Its Commander, William Lamb, Colonel, CSA

The capture of Fort Fisher, N.C., on the 15th of January 1865, was followed so quickly by the final dissolution of the Southern Confederacy that the great victory was not fully realized by the American people. The position commanded the last gateway between the Confederate States and the outside world. Its capture, with the resulting loss of all the Cape Fear River defenses, and of Wilmington, the great importing depot of the South, effectually ended all blockade running. Lee sent me word that Fort Fisher must be held, or he could not subsist his army.

The indentation of the Atlantic Ocean in the Carolina coast known as Onslow Bay and the Cape Fear River running south from Wilmington form the peninsula known as Federal Point, which, during the civil war, was called Confederate Point. Not quite seven miles north of the end of this peninsula stood a high sand-hill called the "Sugar Loaf." Here there was an intrenched camp for the Army of Wilmington, under General Braxton Bragg, the department commander, that was hid from the sea by forest and sand-hills. From this intrenched camp the riverbank, with a neighboring ridge of sand-dunes, formed a covered way for troops to within a hundred yards of the left salient of Fort Fisher. Between this road and the ocean beach was an arm of Masonboro Sound and where it ended, three miles north of the fort, were occasional fresh-water swamps, generally wooded with scrub growth, and in many places quite impassable. Along the ocean shore was an occasional battery formed from a natural sand-hill, behind which Whitworth guns were carried from the fort to cover belated blockade-runners, or to protect more unfortunate ones that had been chased ashore. About half a mile north of the fort there was a rise in the plain forming a hill some twenty feet above the tide on the river side, and on this was a redoubt commanding the approach to the fort by the river road. Thus Nature, assisted by some slight engineering work, had given a defense to Confederate Point which would have enabled an efficient commander at the intrenched camp, cooperating with the garrison of Fort Fisher, to have rendered the Point untenable for a largely superior force at night when the covering fire of the Federal navy could not distinguish between friend and foe.

At the land-face of Fort Fisher, five miles from the intrenched camp, the peninsula was about half a mile wide. This face commenced about a hundred feet from the river with a half bastion, and extended with a heavy curtain to a full bastion on the ocean side, where it joined the sea-face.[14] The work

---

[14]When I assumed command of Fort Fisher, July 4th, 1862, it was composed of several detached earth-works, with a casemated battery of sand and palmetto logs, mounting; four guns and with only one heavy gun in the works. The frigate *Minnesota* could have destroyed the works and driven us out in a few hours. I immediately went to work, and with 500 colored laborers, assisted by the garrison, constructed the largest earthwork in the Southern Confederacy, of heavy timbers covered by sand from 15 to 20 feet deep and sodded with turf. The fort was far from complete when it was attacked, especially as against an assault by land; the sides exposed to the sea being first constructed, on the theory that the Army of Wilmington would prevent an investment.—W.L.

was built to withstand the heaviest artillery fire. There was no moat with scarp and counterscarp, so essential for defense against storming parties, the shifting sands rendering its construction impossible with the material available. The outer slope was twenty feet high from the berme to the top of the parapet, at an angle of 45 degrees and was sodded with marsh grass, which grew luxuriantly. The parapet was not less than twenty-five feet thick, with an inclination of only one foot. The revetment was five feet nine inches high from the floor of the gun-chambers, and these were some twelve feet or more from the interior plane. The guns were all mounted in barbette, on Columbiad carriages; there was not a single casemated gun in the fort. Experience had taught that casemates of timber and sand-bags were a delusion and a snare against heavy projectiles; and there was no iron to construct them with. Between the gun-chambers, containing one or two guns each (there were twenty heavy guns on the land-face), there were heavy traverses, exceeding in size any known to engineers, to protect from an enfilading fire. They extended out some twelve feet on the parapet, and were twelve feet or more in height above the parapet, running back thirty feet or more. The gun-chambers were reached from the rear by steps. In each traverse was an alternate magazine or bomb-proof, the latter ventilated by an air-chamber. Passageways penetrated the traverses in the interior of the work, forming additional bomb-proofs for the reliefs for the guns.

The sea-face for a hundred yards from the northeast bastion was of the same massive character as the land-face. A crescent battery, intended for four guns, joined this. It had been originally built of palmetto logs and tarred sandbags and sand revetted with sod; but the logs had decayed, and it was converted into a hospital bomb-proof. In its rear a heavy curtain was thrown up to protect the chambers from fragments of shells. From this bomb-proof a series of batteries extended for three-quarters of a mile along the sea, connected by an infantry curtain. These batteries had heavy traverses, but were not more than ten or twelve feet high to the top of the parapets, and were built for ricochet firing. On this line was a bomb-proof electric battery connected with a system of submarine torpedoes. Farther along, where the channel ran close to the beach, inside the bar, a mound battery 60 feet high was erected, with two heavy guns, which had a plunging fire on the channel; this was connected with the battery north of it by a light curtain. Following the line of the works, it was over one mile from the mound to the north-east bastion at the angle of the sea and land faces, and upon this line twenty-four heavy guns were mounted. From the mound for nearly a mile to the end of the point was a level sand-plain scarcely three feet above high tide, and much of it was submerged during gales. At the point was Battery Buchanan, four guns, in the shape of an ellipse, commanding the inlet, its two 11-inch guns covering the approach by land. It was garrisoned by a detachment from the Confederate States navy. An advanced redoubt with a 24-pounder was added after the attack by the forces under General Butler and Admiral Porter on Christmas, 1864. A wharf for large steamers was in close proximity to these works. Battery Buchanan was a citadel to which an overpowered garrison might retreat and with proper transportation be safely carried off at night, and to which reënforcements could be sent under the cover of darkness.

Thus Fort Fisher, being designed to withstand the heaviest bombardment, was extremely difficult to defend against assault after its guns were destroyed. The soldiers in the gun-chambers could not see the approach in front for a hundred feet, and to repel assailants they had to leave all cover and stand upon the open parapet.

As a defense against infantry there was a system of sub-terra torpedoes extending across the peninsula, five to six hundred feet from the land-face, and so disconnected that the explosion of one would not affect the others; inside the torpedoes, about fifty feet from the berme of the work, extending from river bank to sea-shore, was a heavy palisade of sharpened logs nine feet high pierced for musketry, and so laid out as to have an enfilading fire on the center, where there was a redoubt, guarding a sally-port, from which two Napoleons were run out, as occasion required. At the river end of the palisade was a deep and muddy slough, across which was a bridge, the entrance of the river road into the fort; commanding this bridge was a Napoleon gun. There were three mortars in rear of the land-face.

It was after a careful reconnaissance on December 25th, 1864, having drawn our fire by an advance of his skirmish-line to within 75 yards of the fort, that General Godfrey Weitzel, finding the works substantially uninjured by the explosion of the powder-ship and the two days' terrific bombardment of Porter's great armada, reported to Butler that the fort could not be carried by assault.[15] In the works on that afternoon were over 900 veteran troops and

---

[15]General B. F. Butler in his report of the operations of his troops, says in part: "Brevet Brigadier-General [N. M.] Curtis, who deserves well for his gallantry and conduct, immediately pushed up his brigade within a few hundred yards of Fort Fisher, capturing the Half-moon battery and its men, who were taken off by the boats of the navy. In the meantime the remainder of Ames's division had captured 218 men and 10 commissioned officers of the North Carolina reserves and other prisoners. From them I learned that Kirkland's and Hagood's brigades of Hoke's division had left the front of the Army of the James, near Richmond, and were then within two miles of the rear of my forces, and their skirmishers were then actually engaged, and that the remainder of Hoke's division had come the night before to Wilmington, and were then on the march, if they had not already arrived. General Weitzel reported that to assault the work, in his judgment, and in that of the experienced officers of his command who had been on the skirmish-line, with any prospect of success, was impossible. This opinion coincided with my own, and much as I regretted the necessity of abandoning the attempt, yet the path of duty was plain. Not so strong a work as Fort Fisher had been taken by assault during

450 junior reserves, reënforced after dark by 60 sailors and marines. As soon as the fire of the fleet ceased, the parapets were not only manned, but half the garrison was stationed outside the work behind the palisades. There was no fear of an assault in front; what most disturbed the defenders was a possible landing from boats between the Mound Battery and Battery Buchanan. Admiral Porter was as much to blame as General Butler for the repulse.[16]

The garrison of Fort Fisher was composed altogether of North Carolinians. For two years and a half the force had been under my command, and in that time only two companies, temporarily there, were from outside the State. After the repulse of Butler and Porter, although some important guns were destroyed by the bombardment and by explosion, little or nothing was done to repair damages or strengthen the armament of the work. Requisitions were made for additional ammunition, especially for hand-grenades, to repel assault, but it was impossible to obtain what was needed. Application was made for the placing of marine torpedoes where the iron-clads had anchored, and whither they returned, but no notice was taken of it. Although we heard on January 8th that the fleet had returned to Beaufort, and we knew that Fort

---

the war, and I had to guide me the experience of Port Hudson, with its slaughtered thousands in the repulsed assault, and the double assault of Fort Wagner, where thousands were sacrificed in an attempt to take a work less strong than Fisher, after it had been subjected to a more continued and fully as severe fire. And in neither of the instances I have mentioned had the assaulting force in its rear, as I had, an army of the enemy larger than itself. I therefore ordered that no assault should be made, and that the troops should reembark."—Editors.

[16]General Butler was blamed by contemporaneous writers for not capturing the works. For this criticism he had himself to blame. On the evening of the 25th, before waiting for official reports, he listened to camp gossip and wrote to Admiral Porter: "General Weitzel advanced his skirmish-line within fifty yards of the fort, while the garrison was kept in their bomb-proofs by the fire of the navy, and so closely that three or four men of the picket-line ventured upon the parapet and through the sally-port of the work, capturing a horse, which they brought off, killing the orderly, who was the bearer of a dispatch from the chief of artillery of General Whiting, to bring a light battery within the fort, and also brought away from the parapet the flag of the fort." This piece of romance was sent North, and has gotten a lodgment in current history, and is actually repeated by General Grant in his "Memoirs," though General Butler corrected the error in his official report of January 3d, 1865. No Federal soldier entered Fort Fisher Christmas day, except as a prisoner. The courier was sent out of the fort without my knowledge, and was killed and his horse captured within the enemy's lines.

The flag captured was a small company flag, placed on the extreme left of the work, and which was carried away and thrown off the parapet by an enfilading shot from the navy. It was during a terrific bombardment of the land-face when I had ordered my men to cover themselves behind parapet and traverses as well as in the bomb-proofs. Amid the smoke of bursting shells, Captain W. H. Walling, of the 142d New York, gallantly crawled through the broken palisade and carried off the flag, doing what two or more men could not have done without observation. The angle of the work hid him from the sharp-shooters on the front, who, from behind traverses, were watching for an advance.

When Butler's skirmish-line approached I purposely withheld the fire of infantry and artillery until an attack should be made in force. Only one gun on the land face had been seriously disabled, and I could have opened a fire of grape and canister on the narrow beach, which no troops could have survived. In the second attack by the army, as the reader will see, all my heavy guns on the land-face but one were disabled; my torpedoes were useless, and my palisades were so torn up and cut down that they furnished a protection to the assailants instead of a formidable impediment.—W.L.

Fisher was still its objective point, General Braxton Bragg withdrew the supporting army from Sugar Loaf and marched it to a camp sixteen miles distant, north of Wilmington, and there had a grand review. The fort was not even advised of the coming of the fleet, which should have been seen off Masonboro during the day; and its arrival was reported from Fort Fisher to headquarters in Wilmington.

The night of the 12th of January, from the ramparts of Fort Fisher, I saw the great armada returning. My mounted pickets had informed me of its coming. I began at once to put my works in order for action. I had but 800 men—the 36th North Carolina—at least 100 of whom were not fit for duty. Sunrise the next morning revealed to us the most formidable armada the world had ever known, supplemented by transports carrying about 8500 troops. Suddenly that long line of floating fortresses rained shot and shell, upon fort and beach and wooded hills, causing the very earth and sea to tremble. I had telegraphed for reënforcement, and during the day and night following about 700 arrived—companies of light and heavy artillery, North Carolina troops, and some 50 sailors and marines of the Confederate States navy—giving me 1500, all told, up to the morning of January 15th, including the sick and slightly wounded. On Friday, the 13th in the midst of the bombardment, General W. H. C. Whiting, the district commander, and his staff, arrived in the fort. They had walked up from Battery Buchanan. I did not know of their approach until the general came to me on the works and remarked, "Lamb, my boy, I have come to share your fate. You and your garrison are to be sacrificed." I replied, "Don't say so, General; we shall certainly whip the enemy again." He then told me that when he left Wilmington General Bragg was hastily removing his stores and ammunition, and was looking for a place to fall back upon.[17] I offered him the command, although he came unarmed and without orders; but he refused, saying he would counsel with me, but would leave me to conduct the defense.

In the former bombardment the fire of the fleet had been diffuse, not calculated to effect any particular damage, and so wild that at least one-third of the missiles fell in the river beyond the fort or in the bordering marshes; but now the fire was concentrated, and the definite object of the fleet was

---

[17]In a report to General Lee dictated at Fort Fisher January 18, 1865, and in another (enclosing the first one) dated Fort Columbus, New York Harbor, February 19, 1865, General Whiting blames General Bragg for the loss of Fort Fisher, and asks that the latter's conduct be investigated. He says: "I went into the fort with the conviction that it was to be sacrificed, for the last I heard General Bragg say, was to point out a line to fall back on if Fort Fisher fell." General Bragg was "charged with the command and defense of Wilmington," by the Secretary of War, on January 13; and General Whiting concludes with a feeling reference to the fact that he was not allowed to conduct the defense of "a harbor on which I had expended for two years all the labor and skill I had."—Editors.

the destruction of the land defenses by enfilade and direct fire, and the ships took position accordingly. When attacked in December, I had had for my 44 heavy guns and three mortars not over 3600 shot and shell; and for the most effective gun in the work, the 150-pounder Armstrong, there were but 13 shells, and we had no other ammunition that could be used in it. The frigates *Minnesota* and *Wabash* each had an armament superior to ours, and these two vessels alone fired more shot and shell at the works in the last attack than we had, all told or on hand, in both engagements. During the time between the two expeditions we had begged for more ammunition, but none came except a few useless bolts designed for the Armstrong gun. In the former fight we had fired 1272 shot and shell; leaving about 2328, exclusive of grape and shrapnel, to resist a passage of the ships and an assault by land. I was obliged to husband my ammunition even more than in the previous battle, and therefore gave the same orders that each gun should be fired only once every half-hour until disabled or destroyed, except when special orders were given to concentrate on a particular vessel, or in case an attempt were made to cross the bar and run in, when every available gun should be used with all possible effectiveness. It was this slow firing from the fort, at times not over forty-four guns in thirty minutes, compared to the naval fire of from one to two guns a second, that gave the navy the erroneous idea that they had silenced the fort. But no attempt was made to run by the fort, which was a great surprise to us. Occasionally a wooden vessel, more daring than her consorts, would come close in, when the guns of several batteries would be concentrated upon her and she would be quickly withdrawn more or less injured.

All day and night on the 13th and 14th of January the navy continued its ceaseless torment; it was impossible to repair damages at night on the land-face. The *Ironsides* and monitors bowled their eleven and fifteen inch shells along the parapet, scattering shrapnel in the darkness. We could scarcely gather up and bury our dead without fresh casualties. At least two hundred had been killed and wounded in the two days since the fight began. Only three or four of my land guns were of any service. The Federal army had been approaching on the river side during the day; but they were more or less covered by the formation of the land, and we could only surmise their number. I had seen them pass Craig's Landing near my cottage and occupy the redoubt about half a mile from the fort. We had fired some shot and shell at their approaching columns, but it was at a fearful cost of limb and life that a land gun was discharged; for to fire from that face was to draw upon the gunners the fury of the fleet. Early in the afternoon, to my astonishment, I saw a Confederate flat-bottomed steam-transport, loaded with stores, approaching Craig's Landing, which was now in the enemy's lines. I had a gun fired toward her to warn her off, but on she came, unconscious of her danger, and she fell an easy captive in the enemy's hands. Shortly after, the Confederate steamer *Chickamauga*, which had been annoying the enemy from the river, fired into and sank the stupid craft. This incident gave me the first intimation that we were deserted. From the conformation of the Cape Fear River, General Bragg could have passed safely from Sugar Loaf toward Smithfield, and with a glass could have seen everything on the beach and in the fort, and in person or through an aide, with the steamers at his command, could have detected every movement of the enemy; but now, thirty-six hours after the fight had commenced, several hours after Craig's Landing had been in the possession of the enemy, he sent into the enemy's lines a steamer full of sorely needed stores, which at night could have gone to Battery Buchanan in safety. We had both tele-graphic and signal communication between Fort Fisher and Sugar Loaf, Bragg's headquarters, and I got General Whiting to telegraph him to attack the enemy under cover of night when the fleet could not cooperate, and we would do the same from the fort, and that thus we could capture a portion or the whole of the force, or at least demoralize it. No reply was received. Still I thought General Bragg could not fail to respond; so, after the dead were buried, ten companies were put in readiness for a sortie, and I carried Captain Patterson's company out in front of the work beyond the palisade line and the range of the enemy's fire, and threw them out as skirmishers with orders to discover the position of the enemy. We found none on the sea-shore within half a mile, but on the river-shore they were occupying the redoubt, where their skirmishers extended toward the left of the fort. Some of them fired on us, but we remained there awaiting a message from Bragg, or the sound of his guns from the north but in vain, and before daylight we retired to the fort.

With the rising sun, on the 15th, the fleet, which had been annoying us all through the night, redoubled its fire on the land-face. The sea was calm, the naval gunners had become accurate by practice, and before noon but one heavy gun, protected by the angle of the north-east bastion, remained serviceable on that face. The harvest of wounded and dead was increased, and at noon I had not 1200 men to defend the long line of works. The enemy were now preparing to assault; we saw their skirmish-line on the left digging riflepits close to our torpedo lines and their columns along the river-shore massing for the attack, while their sharp-shooters were firing upon every head that showed itself upon our front. Despite the imminent danger to the gunners I ordered the two Napoleons at the central sally-port and the Napoleon on the left to fire grape and canister upon the advancing skirmish-line.

They fearlessly obeyed with effectiveness, but at a sad sacrifice in killed and wounded. At the same time on the ocean side a column composed of sailors and marines was seen to approach, the advance throwing up slight trenches. On these we brought to bear our single heavy gun, while the two guns on the mound battery turned their attention from the sailors afloat to the sailors on shore, but at too long range to be very effective. Hagood's brigade, sent by Bragg, was now arriving at Battery Buchanan, but the steamer bearing them was driven off by the fire of the fleet after it had succeeded in landing two South Carolina regiments, which came at a double-quick to the mound under a heavy fire. The number of these reënforcements was reported to me by the officer in command as 350. They reached the fort less than thirty minutes before the attacking columns came like avalanches upon our right and left. The South Carolinians were out of breath and more or less disorganized and demoralized by the ordeal through which, by Bragg's neglect, they had been forced to pass. I sent them to an old commissary bomb-proof to recover breath.

My headquarters during the fight were the pulpit battery on the sea-face, one hundred yards from the north-east salient and adjoining the hospital bomb-proof, commanding the best view of the approaches to the land-face. At half-past two, as I was returning from another battery, Private Arthur Muldoon, one of my lookouts, called to me, "Colonel, the enemy are about to charge." I informed General Whiting, who was near, and at my request he immediately telegraphed General Bragg, at "Sugar Loaf": "The enemy are about to assault; they outnumber us heavily. We are just manning our parapets. Fleet have extended down the sea-front outside and are firing very heavily. Enemy on the beach in front of us in very heavy force, not more than seven hundred yards from us. Nearly all land guns disabled. Attack! Attack! It is all I can say and all you can do."[18]

I then passed hurriedly down in rear of the land-face and through the galleries, and although the fire of the fleet was terrific, I knew it must soon cease, and I ordered additional sharp-shooters to the gun-chambers with instructions to pick off the officers in the assaulting columns, and directed the battery commanders to form their detachments and rush to the top of the parapets when the firing stopped and drive the assailants back. As I returned, I instructed the squads that were forming under cover to rally to the parapets as soon as the order should be given, to which they responded with enthusiasm. I had determined to allow the assailants to reach the berme of the work

---

[18]The original, in Whiting's handwriting, is in possession of Dr. Geo. L. Porter, Bridgeport, Conn.—W.L.

before exploding a line of torpedoes, believing it would enable us to kill or capture the first line, while destroying or demoralizing their supporting lines of assault. I had not quite reached my headquarters when the roar of artillery suddenly ceased, and instantly the steam-whistles of the vast fleet sounded a charge. It was a soul-stirring signal both to besiegers and besieged.

I ordered my aide, Lieutenant Charles H. Blocker, to double-quick the 21st and 25th South Carolina to reenforce Major James Reilly, whom I had put in command on the left, while I went to the northeast salient, which I believed to be the vital point of the work and the one which needed most protection. I rallied there the larger portion of the garrison of the main work, putting 300 men on top of the bastion and adjoining parapets and holding some 200 more in the adjoining batteries. About 250 remained for defense on the left, to which I supposed the 350 South Carolinians would immediately be added, and these with the Napoleon and the torpedoes I felt sure would successfully defend that portion of the work. The assaulting line on the right was directed at the angle or point of the L, and consisted of two thousand sailors and marines,[19] the greater portion of whom had flanked my torpedo lines by keeping close to the sea. Ordering the mound battery, and any other on the sea-face that could do so, to fire upon them, and the two Napoleons at the sally-port to join our Columbiad in pouring grape and canister into their ranks, I held in reserve the infantry fire. Whiting stood upon the brink of the parapet inspiring those about him. The sailors and marines reached the berme and some sprang up the slope, but a murderous fire greeted them and swept them down. Volley after volley was poured into their faltering ranks by cool, determined men, and in half an hour several hundred dead and wounded lay at the foot of the bastion. The bravery of the officers could not restrain their men from panic and retreat, and with small loss to ourselves we witnessed what had never been seen before, a disorderly rout of American sailors and marines. Had the fleet helped their own column as they did afterward that of the army, theirs would have been the glory of victory.

As our shouts of triumph went up I turned to look at the western salient, and saw, to my astonishment, three Federal battle-flags upon our ramparts. General Whiting saw them at the same moment, and, calling on the men to pull down those flags and drive the enemy from the work, rushed toward them on the parapet. Among those who followed Whiting, and who gave his

---

[19]Secretary Welles, in his report of the Navy Department, December 4, 1865, says: "Fourteen hundred sailors and marines were landed and participated in the direct assault"; but Admiral Porter in his report, dated off Fort Fisher, January 17, 1865, says: " I detailed 1600 sailors and 400 marines to accompany the troops in the assault—the sailors to board the sea-face, while the troops assaulted the land side."—Editors.

young life upon those ramparts, I must mention the brave Lieutenant Wil-
liford, who commanded the Blakely battery.

In order to make a careful reconnoissance of the position of the enemy,
I passed through the sally-port, and outside of the work witnessed a savage
hand-to-hand conflict for the possession of the fourth gun-chamber from the
left bastion. My men, led by Whiting, had driven the standard-bearer from
the top of the traverse and the enemy from the parapet in front. They had
recovered the gun-chamber with great slaughter, and on the parapet and
on the long traverse of the next gun chamber the contestants were savagely
firing into each other's faces, and in some cases clubbing their guns, being
too close to load and fire. Whiting had quickly been wounded by two shots
and had been carried to the hospital bomb-proof. I saw that the Confederates were exposed not only to the fire in front, but to a galling infantry fire
from the captured salient. I saw also a fresh force pouring into the left of the
work, now offering no resistance. I doubt if ever before the commander of a
work went outside of it and looked back upon the conflict for its possession;
but from the peculiar construction of the works it was necessary to do so in
order to see the exact position of affairs. I was in front of the sally-port and
concealed from the army by a fragment of the palisade.[20]

Ordering Captain Z. T. Adams to turn his Napoleons on the column
moving into the fort (the gallant Mayo had already turned his Columbiad
upon them), I returned into the work, and, placing men behind every cover
that could be found, poured at close range a deadlier fire into the flank of
the enemy occupying the gun-chambers and traverses than they were able
to deliver upon my men from the left salient. While thus engaged I met my
aide, who informed me that the South Carolinians had failed to respond to
my order, although their officers had pleaded with them, and with a few of
them had gone into the fight; that the assaulting column had made two distinct charges upon the extreme left and had been repulsed by the fire of the
Napoleon and by the infantry; that the torpedo wires had been cut by the fire
of the fleet and the electrician had tried in vain to execute my orders; that,
driven from the extreme left, the enemy had found a weak defense between
the left salient and the sally-port in their third charge, and had gained the
parapet and, capturing two gun-chambers, had attacked the force in the left
bastion on the flank simultaneously with a direct charge of a fresh column,

---

[20]I was told, several years after the war, by a United States marine named Clark, that I was
distinctly seen and recognized by a comrade and himself who had feigned death in front of the
north-east salient, and that his comrade rose from his place of concealment to shoot me but before
he could fire was shot in the head by a soldier in the fort. I never thought of danger from that direction.—W.L.

and that our men after great slaughter, especially those at the Napoleon, had been forced to surrender just as we had repulsed the naval column; that to add to the discomfiture of the Confederates, as soon as the Federal battle-flags appeared on the ramparts, Battery Buchanan had opened with its two heavy guns on the left of the work, killing and wounding friend and foe alike. Major Reilly had failed to lead the men to the top of the parapet on the right of the western salient, firing instead from the two gun-chambers on the assailants, who were not within range until they reached the parapet. Had the parapet been manned by fifty determined men at this point, I do not believe the enemy could have got into the fort before reënforcements had arrived. Reilly was a veteran soldier, and showed his indomitable courage later in the day, but his mistake was fatal. This was disheartening, but I told Captain Blocker if we could hold the enemy in check until dark I would then drive them out, and I sent a telegram by him to Bragg, imploring him to attack, and saying that I could still save the fort.

Notwithstanding the loss of a portion of the work and a part of the garrison, the men were in good spirits and seemed determined to recover the fort. We had retaken one gun-chamber in the charge on the parapet, and since we had opened on their flank we had shot down all their standard-bearers, and the Federal battle-flags had disappeared from our ramparts. I was encouraged to believe that before sundown we could recover all the gun-chambers to the east of the western salient. Just as the tide of battle seemed to have turned in our favor the remorseless fleet came to the rescue of the faltering Federals. Suddenly the bombardment, which had been confined to the sea face, turned again on our land-front, and with deadly precision; the iron-clads and heavy frigates drove in our Napoleons and exploded shells in the interior of the sally-port, which had heretofore escaped. They also swept the gun-chamber occupied by Confederates in front of those occupied by the enemy, and their shells rolled down within the works and exploded in most unexpected quarters, preventing even company formation. They drove from the front of the enemy all assailants except those so near that to have fired on them would have been to slaughter the Federals.

We had now to contend with a column advancing around the rear of the left bastion into the interior plane of the fort. It moved slowly and cautiously, apparently in column of companies and in close order. I met it with an effective infantry fire, my men using the remains of an old work as a breastwork and taking advantage of every object that would afford cover, for we were now greatly outnumbered. The fire was so unexpected and destructive on the massed columns of the Federals that they halted when an advance would have been fatal to us. With orders to the officers to dispute stubbornly any advance until my return, I went rapidly to the extreme southern limit of my work and turned the two mound guns on the column in the fort. As I passed the different batteries I ordered the guns turned on the assailants but on returning, found that only two besides those on the mound would bear upon them, and these had to be fired over my men. I ordered them, notwithstanding, to be fired carefully with properly cut fuses, which was done, but it made some of my men very nervous. I brought back with me to the front every man except a single detachment for each gun. I was gone from the front at least thirty minutes, and on my return found the fighting still continuing over the same traverse for the possession of the gun-chamber, despite the fire of the fleet. As my men would fall others would take their places. It was a soldier's fight at that point, for there could be no organization; the officers of both forces were loading and firing with their men. If there has ever been a longer or more stubborn hand-to hand encounter, I have failed to meet with it in history. The Federal column inside had advanced no farther, and seemed demoralized by the fire of the artillery and the determined resistance of the garrison. I had brought back with me more than a hundred of my old garrison, and I threw them in front with those already engaged. Those who had been driven from the parapet had taken position behind the old work. I went to the bomb-proof where the South Carolinians were and appealed to them to help save the fort; they were in a position to flank a part of the column, and they promised to do so. I proceeded to the sally-port and ordered the gallant Adams to bring his guns out and open fire on the head of the column, and if he had not men left to serve the guns to get volunteers from other companies. I went along the galleries and begged the sick and wounded who had retreated from the captured bomb-proofs to come and make one supreme effort to dislodge the enemy. As I passed through my work the last time, the scene was indescribably horrible. Great cannon were broken in two, and over their ruins were lying the dead; others were partly buried in graves dug by the shells which had slain them.

Still no tidings from Bragg. The enemy's advance had ceased entirely; protected by the fleet, they held the parapet and gun-chambers, but their massed columns refused to move and appeared to be intrenching in the work. I believed a determined assault with the bayonet upon their front would drive them out. I had cautioned the gunners not to fire on our men, and had sent Lieutenant Jones, of the navy, to Battery Buchanan, asking for all the force they could spare, and to be careful not to fire on us if we became closely engaged with the enemy. The head of the column was not over one hundred feet from the portion of our breastwork which I occupied; I passed quickly in rear of the line and asked the officers and men if they would follow me; they all responded fearlessly that they would. I returned to my post, and, giving the order "Charge bayonets," sprang upon the breastwork, waved my sword, and, as I gave the command "Forward! double-quick, march!" fell on my knees, a rifle-ball having entered my left hip. We were met by a heavy volley, aimed too high to be effective; but our column wavered and fell back behind the breastworks. A soldier raised me up; I turned the command over to Captain Daniel Munn and told him to keep the enemy in check, and that I would bandage my wound and soon return. Before I could reach the hospital I was made to realize that I was incapacitated from joining my men again. In the hospital I found General Whiting suffering uncomplainingly from his two wounds. He told me that Bragg had ignored his presence in the fort and had not noticed his messages. I perceived that the fire of my men had slackened, and sent my acting adjutant, John N. Kelly, for Major Reilly, next in command (Major James M. Stevenson being too ill for service). Reilly came and promised me that he would continue the fight as long as a man or a shot was left, and nobly did he keep his promise. I again sent a message to Bragg begging him to come to the rescue. Shortly after my fall the Federals made an advance, and, capturing several more of the gun-chambers, reached the sally-port. The column in the work advanced, but Major Reilly, rallying the men, among them the South Carolinians, who had all become engaged, drove them back. About 8 o'clock at night my aide came to me and said the ammunition was giving out; that he and Chaplain McKinnon had gathered all on the dead and wounded in a blanket and had distributed it; that the enemy had possession of nearly all of the land-face; that it was impossible to hold out much longer, and suggested that it would be wise to surrender, as a further struggle might be a useless sacrifice of life. I replied that so long as I lived I would not surrender the fort; that Bragg must soon come to the rescue, and it would save us. General Whiting remarked, "Lamb, when you die I will assume command, and I will not surrender the fort." In less than an hour a fourth brigade (three were already in the fort under General Ames) entered the sally-port and swept the defenders from the remainder of the land-face. Major Reilly had General Whiting and myself hurriedly removed on stretchers to Battery Buchanan, where he purposed to make a stand. When we left the hospital the men were fighting over the adjoining traverse and the spent balls fell like hail-stones around us. The garrison then fell back in an orderly retreat along the sea face, the rear-guard keeping the enemy engaged as they advanced slowly and cautiously in the darkness as far as the Mound Battery, where they halted. Some of the men, cut off from the main body, had to retreat as best they could over the river marsh, while some few unarmed artillerists barely eluded the enemy by following the seashore. When we reached Battery Buchanan there was a mile of level beach between us and our pursuers, swept by two 11-inch guns and a 24-pounder and in close proximity to the battery, a commodious wharf where transports could have come to carry the men off. We expected to cover with this battery the retreat of the remnant of the garrison, but we found the guns spiked, and every means of transportation, even the barge and crew of the colonel commanding, taken by Captain R. F. Chapman, of our navy, who, following the example of General Bragg, had abandoned us to our fate. None of the guns of Fort Fisher were spiked, the men fighting them until they were destroyed or their defenders were killed, wounded, or driven out of the batteries by overwhelming numbers. The enemy threw out a heavy skirmish-line and sent their fourth brigade to Battery Buchanan, where it arrived about 10 P.M. and received the surrender of the garrison from Major James H. Hill and Lieutenant George D. Parker. Some fifteen minutes or more before the surrender, while lying on a stretcher near General Whiting in front of the battery, and witnessing the grand pyrotechnic display of the fleet over the capture of Fort Fisher, I was accosted by General A. H. Colquitt, who had been ordered to the fort to take command. I had a few moments' hurried conversation with him, informed him of the assault, of the early loss of a portion of the work and garrison, and that when I fell it had for a time demoralized the men, but that the enemy was equally demoralized by our unexpected resistance; and I assured him that if Bragg would even then attack, a fresh brigade landed at Battery Buchanan could retake the work. Some officer suggested that the general should take me with him, as I was probably fatally wounded, but I refused to leave, wishing to share the fate of my garrison; and desiring that my family, anxiously awaiting tidings across the river, where they had watched the battle, should not be alarmed, I spoke lightly of my wound. I asked him to carry General Whiting to a place of safety, as he had come to the fort a volunteer. Just then the approach of the enemy was reported, and Colquitt made a precipitate retreat, leaving Whiting behind.[21]

One more distressing scene remains to be chronicled. The next morning after sunrise a frightful explosion occurred in my reserve magazine, killing and wounding several hundred of the enemy and some of my own wounded officers and men. The magazine was a frame structure 20 x 60 feet and 6 feet high, covered with 18 feet or more of sand, luxuriantly turfed, and contained probably 13,000 pounds of powder. It made an artificial mound most inviting to a wearied soldier, and after the fight was occupied for the night by Colonel Alden's 169th New York and by some of my suffering soldiers. Two sailors from the fleet, stupefied by liquor which they had found in the hospital, and

---

[21]General Whiting died a prisoner at Fort Columbus, New York Harbor, March 10, 1865. [Attribution missing.]

looking for booty, were seen to enter the structure with lights, and a moment after the green mound blew up. The telegraph wires, running from a bomb-proof near this magazine across the river to Battery Lamb, gave rise to the impression that it had been purposely exploded from the opposite shore, but an official investigation traced it to the drunken sailors.

So stoutly did those works resist the 50,000 shot and shell thrown against them in the two bombardments that not a magazine or bomb-proof was injured, and after the land armament, with palisades and torpedoes, had been destroyed, no assault would have been practicable in the presence of Bragg's force, had it been under a competent officer.[22] One thousand tons of iron were gathered by the United States from the works. Had there been no fleet to assist the army at Fort Fisher the Federal infantry could not have dared assault it until its land defenses had been destroyed by gradual approaches. For the first time in the history of sieges the land defenses of the works were destroyed, not by any act of the besieging army, but by the concentrated fire, direct and enfilading, of an immense fleet poured upon them without intermission, until torpedo wires were cut, palisades breached so that they actually afforded cover for assailants, and the slopes of the work were rendered practicable for assault.

---

[22]In Vol. X., p. 346, of the *Southern Historical Society Papers* may be found a letter from General Braxton Bragg to his brother, dated Wilmington, five days after the fall of Fort Fisher (first published in 1881); also an article by Colonel Lamb, controverting most of General Bragg's statements. General Bragg says (more emphatically but substantially as in his official report): "Two hours before hearing of the certain fall of the fort, I felt as confident as ever man did of successfully defending it. . . . No human power could have prevented the enemy from landing, covered as he was by a fleet of ships carrying 600 heavy guns. Anywhere beyond the range of our heavy guns on the fort our land force could not approach him. Once landed, our only chance was to keep him, if possible, from the fort. With less than half his numbers, had we extended far enough toward the fort to prevent his movement that way he could have crossed the narrow peninsula north of us and cut us off entirely, when the fort and all must have gone."

General Bragg, after explaining that his cavalry pickets failed to report the movement by night of Terry's force to its entrenched position near Fort Fisher, says: "I put the command in motion, and ordered the enemy dislodged if it was at all practicable. General Hoke and his brigadiers made a close reconnoissance and expressed to me the opinion that their troops were unequal to the task. I moved forward with them, and made a close examination, confirmed their opinion, and after a conference decided not to attack. An attack and failure would have insured the fall of the fort, and would also have opened the whole State. We could not have succeeded without defeating double our numbers behind intrenchments, while at the same time exposed to a raking fire from their fleet. . . . Believing myself that Grant's army could not storm and carry the fort if it was defended, I felt perfect confidence that the enemy had assumed a most precarious position, from which he would escape with great difficulty. I accordingly ordered Hoke to intrench immediately in his front, and push his lines close on him so as to keep him engaged and closely observed. . . . Had the cavalry done its duty and promptly reported the enemy's movements, I do not think the result would have been different. Such was the configuration of the country and the obstacles, that he would have accomplished his object with the force he had. Our only safe reliance was in his repulse, we being the weak and assailed party. . . . The defense of the fort ought to have been successful against this attack, but it had to fall eventually. The expedition brought against it was able to reduce it in spite of all I could do."—Editors.

The Navy at Fort Fisher

By Thomas O. Selfridge Jr., Captain, USN

When the Secretary of the Navy, Mr. Welles, recognizing the importance of closing the port of Wilmington, urged upon President Lincoln to direct a co-operation of the army, General Grant was requested to supply the necessary force from the troops about Richmond. As Fort Fisher lay within the territorial jurisdiction of General Butler, commanding the Department of Virginia and North Carolina, the troops were detailed from his command, and in the first attack Butler, with General Weitzel in immediate command of the troops, had control of the land operations. The naval command of the expedition having been declined by Admiral Farragut, on account of ill-health, Rear-Admiral Porter, who had so successfully cooperated with the army in opening the Mississippi, was selected, and was allowed to bring with him five of his officers, of whom the writer was one, being detailed for the command of the gun-boat *Huron*. The Atlantic and Gulf coasts being almost entirely in our possession, the Navy Department was able to concentrate before Fort Fisher a larger force than had ever before assembled under one command in the history of the American navy—a total of nearly 60 vessels, of which five were iron-clads, including the *New Ironsides*, besides the three largest of our steam-frigates, viz., the *Minnesota*, *Colorado*, and *Wabash*.[23] The fleet arrived in sight of the fort on the morning of December 20th.

A novel feature of this first attack was the explosion of a powder-boat near the fort on the night of December 23rd. The vessel was the *Louisiana*, an old gun-boat no longer serviceable. The more sanguine believed that Fort Fisher, with its garrison, guns, and equipment, would be leveled to the ground, while others were equally certain it would prove a fizzle. Commander A. C. Rhind, with a crew of volunteers, successfully performed the perilous duty, and, applying the match at midnight, the crew rowed safely away to the *Wilderness*, a swift gun-boat, in waiting. The whole fleet having moved off shore, under low steam, awaited the result in anxiety. A glare on the horizon and a dull report were the indications that the floating mine had been sprung. In the morning, when the fleet steamed in, all eyes were toward the fort. There it was, as grim as ever, apparently uninjured, with its flag floating as defiantly as before. In these days, with better electrical appliances, the explosion could have been made more nearly instantaneous, but I doubt if the general result would have been different.

---

[23]The total number of guns and howitzers in the fleet was over 600, and the total weight of projectiles at a single discharge of all the guns (both broadsides) was over 22 tons.—Editors.

The powder-boat proving an ignominious failure, the fleet stood in toward the fort in close order of divisions, the iron-clads leading. At 11:30 the signal was thrown out from the flag-ship *Malvern*: "Engage the enemy." The *Ironsides*, followed by the monitors, took position as close in as their draught would permit, engaging the north-east face. The *Ironsides* was followed by the *Minnesota*, *Colorado*, and *Wabash*. The enemy replied briskly, but when these frigates found the range and commenced firing rapidly nothing could withstand their broadsides of twenty-five 9-inch guns. It was a magnificent sight to see these frigates fairly engaged, and one never to be forgotten. Their sides seemed a sheet of flame, and the roar of their guns like a mighty thunderbolt. Meanwhile all the other ships took positions as detailed, and so perfect were the plans of the admiral, and so well were they carried out by his captains, that not a mishap took place. Nothing could withstand such a storm of shot and shell as was now poured into this fort. The enemy took refuge in their bomb-proofs, replying sullenly with an occasional gun. The enemy's fire being silenced, signal was made to fire with deliberation, and attention was turned to the dismounting of the guns. So quickly had the guns of Fort Fisher been silenced[24] that not a man had been injured by their fire, though several ships had sustained losses by the bursting of their 100-pounder Parrott rifles. The *Mackinaw*, however, had had her boiler exploded by a shot, and several of her crew had been scalded, and the *Osceola* was struck by a shell near her magazine, but was saved from sinking by her captain, Commander Clitz.

During the bombardment the transports, with troops, arrived from Beaufort. On Christmas day, as agreed upon between Admiral Porter and General Butler, the smaller vessels were engaged in covering the disembarkation of the troops, while the iron-clads and frigates were sent in to resume the bombardment of the fort. The larger portion of the army was landed by the boats of the fleet and advanced with little or no opposition to within a short distance of the fort, the skirmish-line within fifty yards. Butler and Weitzel decided that it could not be taken by assault. Orders were issued to reëmbark

---

[24]In a note to the editors Colonel Lamb says: "The guns of Fort Fisher were not silenced. On account of a limited supply of ammunition, I gave orders to fire each gun not more than once in thirty minutes, except by special order, unless an attempt should be made to run by the fort, when discretion was given each gun commander to use his piece effectively. There were forty-four guns. On the 24th of December 672 shots were expended; a detailed report was received from each battery. Only three guns were rendered unserviceable and these by the fire of the fleet disabling the carriages. On the 25th of December six hundred shots were expended exclusive of grape and canister. Detailed reports were made. Five guns were disabled by the fire of the fleet, making eight in all. Besides, two 7-inch Brooke rifled guns exploded, leaving thirty-four heavy guns on Christmas night. The last guns on the 24th and 25th were fired by Fort Fisher on the retiring fleet. In the first fight the total casualties were 61, as follows: December 24th, mortally wounded, 1; seriously, 3; slightly, 19 = 23. December 25th, killed, 3; mortally wounded, 2; severely, 7; slightly, 26. These included those wounded by the explosion of the Brooke rifled guns = 38."

after being on shore but a few hours. Some seven hundred men were left on shore, the sea being too rough to get them off, but the demoralized enemy did not attempt to attack them. They were taken off in the morning, and the transports steamed away for Hampton Roads, the fleet returning to Beaufort. Thus ended the first attack upon Fort Fisher. Words cannot express the bitter feeling and chagrin of the navy. We all felt the fruit was ripe for plucking and with little exertion would have fallen into the hands of the army.

Second Attack upon Fort Fisher

Upon receiving Admiral Porter's dispatches, Mr. Welles again sought the coöperation of the army, to which General Grant at once acceded, sending back the same force of white troops, reënforced by two colored brigades under General Charles J. Paine, the whole under the command of Major-General Alfred H. Terry. While lying at Beaufort, Admiral Porter determined to assist in the land attack of the army by an assault upon the sea-face of Fort Fisher with a body of seamen. In a general order volunteers from the fleet were called for, and some two thousand officers and men offered themselves for this perilous duty.

General Terry arrived off Beaufort with his forces on the 8th of January 1865, a plan of operations was agreed upon, and the 12th was fixed for the sailing of the combined force.

Upon the morning of the 13th the iron-clads were sent in to engage the fort. Going in much closer than before, the monitors were within twelve hundred yards of the fort. Their fire was in consequence much more effective.

The remainder of the fleet were occupied till 2 P.M. in landing the troops and stores. This particular duty, the provisioning of the army, and the protection of its flank was afterward turned over to the lighter gun-boats, whose guns were too small to employ them in the bombardment of the fort, the whole under the charge of Commander J. H. Upshur, commanding the gunboat A. D. Vance.

On the afternoon of the 13th the fleet, excepting the iron-clads, which had remained in their first positions close to the fort, steamed into the several positions assigned them and opened a terrific fire. By placing a buoy close to the outer reef, as a guide, the leading ship, the Minnesota, was enabled to anchor nearer, and likewise the whole battle-line was much closer and their fire more effective, the best proof of which is the large number of guns upon the land-face of the fort that was found to be destroyed or dismounted.[25] The weight of fire was such that the enemy could make but a feeble reply. At

---

[25]According to the report of General C. B. Comstock, General Terry's chief engineer, there were 21 guns and 3 mortars on the land front; "of these three-fourths were rendered unserviceable." General H. L. Abbot states ("Defense of the Sea Coast of the United States," p. 31), as a result of personal inspection immediately after the capture, that out of 20 guns on the land-face "8 guns and 8 carriages (16 in all) were disabled."—Editors.

nightfall the fleet hauled off, excepting the ironclads, which kept up a slow fire through the night.

During the 14th a number of the smaller gunboats carrying 11-inch guns were sent in to assist in dismounting the guns on the land-face. Their fire was necessarily slow and the presence of these small craft brought the enemy out of their bomb-proofs to open upon them, during which the *Huron* had her main-mast shot away. Upon seeing this renewal of fire the *Brooklyn, Mohican,* and one or two other vessels were ordered in by Porter, and with this reën-forcement the fire of the fort slackened. The bombardment from the smaller gunboats and iron-clads was kept up during the night. This constant duty day and night was very hard upon these small vessels, and the officers and crew of my own vessel, the *Huron,* were worn out.

Fort Fisher was at this time much stronger than at the first attack. The garrison had been reënforced by veteran troops, damages by the first bombardment had been repaired, and new defenses added; among which was a battery of light pieces in a half-moon around the sally-port, from whose fire the sailors suffered heavily in their assault.[26]

It was arranged that the grand bombardment should begin on the morning of the 15th, and the separate assaults of soldiers and sailors should take place at 3 P.M. A code of signals was agreed upon between the two commanders, and the assault was to be signaled to the fleet by a blowing of steam-whistles, whereupon their fire would be directed to the upper batteries. After the assault of the sailors had failed the *Ironsides* used her 11-inch guns with great effect in firing into the traverses filled with Confederates resisting the advance of the Union forces. At 9 A.M. the fleet was directed by signal to move in three divisions, and each ship took its prescribed place as previously indicated to her commander; consequently there was no disorder.

All felt the importance of this bombardment, and while not too rapid to be ineffective such a storm of shell was poured into Fort Fisher that forenoon, as I believe had never been seen before in any naval engagement. The enemy soon ceased to make any reply from their heavy guns, excepting the "Mound Battery," which was more difficult to silence, while those mounted on the land-face were by this time disabled.

Before noon the signal was made for the assaulting column of sailors and marines to land. From thirty-five of the sixty ships of the fleet boats shoved off, making, with their flags flying as they pulled toward the beach in line

---

[26]Colonel Lamb, writing December 1888, says: "There were never in Fort Fisher, including sick, killed, and wounded, over 1900 men. The sailors and marines, etc., captured from Battery Buchanan, and those captured in front of the work, while swelling the list of prisoners, cannot rightly be counted among the defenders of the work. No new defense was added to the face of the fort between the battles. The redoubt in front of the sally-port was there in December and had been used against Butler's skirmish-line."

abreast, a most spirited scene. The general order of Admiral Porter required that the assaulting column of sailors should be armed with cutlasses and pistols. It was also intended that trenches or covered ways should be dug for the marines close to the fort and that our assault should be made under the cover of their fire; but it was impossible to dig such shelter trenches near enough to do much good under fire in broad daylight.

The sailors as they landed from their boats were a heterogeneous assembly, companies of two hundred or more from each of the larger ships, down to small parties of twenty each from the gun-boats. They had been for months confined on shipboard, had never drilled together, and their arms, the old-fashioned cutlass and pistol, were hardly the weapons to cope with the rifles and bayonets of the enemy. Sailor-like, however, they looked upon the landing in the light of a lark, and few thought the sun would set with a loss of one-fifth of their number.

After some discussion between the commander, Lieutenant-Commander K. R. Breese, and the senior officers, it was decided to form three divisions, each composed of the men from the corresponding division squadrons of the fleet; the first division, under the command of Lieutenant-Commander C. H. Cushman, the second under Lieutenant-Commander James Parker (who was Breese's senior but waived his rank, the latter being in command as the admiral's representative), the third under Lieutenant-Commander T. O. Selfridge, Jr.; a total of 1600 blue jackets, to which was added a division of 400 marines under Captain L. L. Dawson.

The whole force marched up the beach and lay down under its cover just outside rifle range, awaiting the movements of the army. We were formed by the flank, and our long line flying numerous flags gave a formidable appearance from the fort, and caused the Confederates to divide their forces, sending more than one-half to oppose the naval assault.

At a preconcerted signal the sailors sprang forward to the assault, closely following the water's edge, where the inclined beach gave them a slight cover. We were opened upon in front by the great mound battery, and in flank by the artillery of the half-moon battery, and by the fire of a thousand rifles. Though many dropped rapidly under this fire, the column never faltered, and when the angle where the two faces of the fort unite was reached the head halted to allow the rear to come up. This halt was fatal, for as the others came up they followed suit and lay down till the space between the parapet and the edge of the water was filled. As the writer approached with the Third Division he shouted to his men to come on, intending to lead them to where there was more space; but, looking back, he discovered that his whole command, with few exceptions, had stopped and joined their comrades. Making his way to the front, close to the palisade, he found several officers, among whom were Lieutenant-Commanders Parker and Cushman. The situation was a very grave one. The rush of the sailors was over; they were packed like sheep in a pen, while the enemy were crowding the ramparts not forty yards away, and shooting into them as fast as they could fire. There was nothing to reply with but *pistols*. Something must be done, and speedily. There were some spaces in the palisade where it was torn away by the fire of the fleet, and an attempt was made to charge through, but we found a deep, impassable ditch,[27] and those who got through were shot down. Flesh and blood could not long endure being killed in this slaughter-pen, and the rear of the sailors broke, followed by the whole body, in spite of all efforts to rally them. It was certainly mortifying, after charging for a mile,[28] under a most galling fire, to the very foot of the fort, to have the whole force retreat down the beach. It has been the custom, unjustly in my opinion, to lay the blame on the marines for not keeping down the fire till the sailors could get in. But there were but 400 of them against 1200 of the garrison: the former in the open plain, and with no cover; the latter under the shelter of their ramparts.[29] The mistake was in expecting a body of sailors, collected hastily from different ships, unknown to each other, armed with swords and pistols, to stand against veteran soldiers armed with rifles and bayonets. Another fatal mistake was the stopping at the sea angle. Two hundred yards farther would have brought us to a low parapet without palisade or ditch, where, with proper arms, we could have intrenched and fought. Some sixty remained at the front, at the foot of the parapet, under cover of the palisade, until nightfall enabled them to withdraw. Among the number I remember Lieutenant-Commanders Breese, Parker, Cushman, Sicard; Lieutenants Farquhar, Lamson, S. W. Nichols, and Bartlett.

A loss of some three hundred in killed and wounded attests the gallant nature of the assault. Among these were several prominent officers, including Lieutenants Preston and Porter, killed; Lieutenant-Commander C. H. Cushman, W. N. Allen, Lieutenant G. M. Bache, wounded.

---

[27]Colonel Lamb says on this point: "There was no ditch, merely a dry depression in front of the berme where sand had been dug out to repair work."—Editors.

[28]General Terry writes that the column of sailors was within 600 or 800 yards of the work before they began to charge; but Commander James Parker says that the column was under fire in marching to that point.—Editors.

[29]Colonel Lamb, writing to the editors on the subject of the numbers defending the north-east salient, says: "Five Hundred effective men will cover all engaged in repulsing the naval column, and the destructive fire was from the three hundred, who, from the top of the ramparts and traverses, fired upon the assailants. The gallant navy need not exaggerate the number opposing them, assisted by the artillery. No apology or defense is necessary to excuse the repulse. The unorganized and improperly armed force failed to enter the fort but their gallant attempt enabled the army to enter and obtain a foothold, which they otherwise could not have done."

After their repulse the sailors did good service with the marines by manning the intrenchments thrown up across the peninsula, which enabled General Terry to send Abbott's brigade and Blackman's (27th U.S.) colored regiment to the assistance of the troops fighting in the fort. Here they remained till morning, when they returned to their respective ships. When the assault of the naval column failed, the *Ironsides* and the monitors were directed to fire into the gun traverses in advance of the positions occupied by the army, and by doing so greatly demoralized the enemy. About 8 P.M. that night the fort fell into our hands after the hardest fighting by our gallant troops, and with its capture fell the last stronghold of the Southern Confederacy on the Atlantic coast.

I will not go so far as to say the army could not have stormed Fort Fisher without the diversion afforded by the naval assault, for no soldiers during the war showed more indomitable pluck than the gallant regiments that stormed the fort on that afternoon; but I do say our attack enabled them to get into the fort with far less loss than they would otherwise have suffered.

As a diversion the charge of sailors was a success; as an exhibition of courage it was magnificent; but the material of which the column was composed, and the arms with which it was furnished, left no reasonable hope after the first onslaught had been checked that it could have succeeded.

While kept under the walls of the fort, I was an eye-witness to an act of heroism on the part of Assistant-Surgeon William Longshaw, a young officer of the medical staff, whose memory should ever be kept green by his corps and which deserves more than this passing notice. A sailor too severely wounded to help himself had fallen close to the water's edge, and with the rising tide would have drowned. Dr. Longshaw, at the peril of his life, went to his assistance and dragged him beyond the incoming tide. At this moment he heard a cry from a wounded marine, one of a small group who, behind a little hillock of sand close to the parapet, kept up a fire upon the enemy. Longshaw ran to his assistance, and while attending to his wounds was shot dead. What made the action of this young officer even more heroic was the fact that on that very day he had received a leave of absence, but had postponed his departure to volunteer for the assault.

APPENDIX 1

Ships Named in the Text

A. D. Vance

Confederate side-wheel blockade-runner. Formerly the Clyde-built packet steamer *Lord Clyde*, she was purchased with funds from private sources and the state of North Carolina. After twenty successful voyages, she was captured on September 10, 1864, off Wilmington, North Carolina, by the blockader *Santiago de Cuba* and taken into the Union navy. She was renamed *Advance* and employed chasing fast blockade-runners. (Cushing referred to the ship in his memoir by its original name.) On April 22, 1865, her name was once more changed, this time to *Frolic*. She continued in active service until decommissioned October 31, 1877. She was sold October 1, 1883. Displacement: 880 tons. Length: 230'. Beam: 26'. Draft: 11' 8''. Complement 107. Speed 12 knots. Armament: four 24-pounder smoothbores; one 20-pounder rifle.

Adelaide

Schooner laden with cotton and turpentine captured and burned in New Topsail Inlet by Cushing while in command of the *Ellis* in October 1862.

Albemarle

Ironclad ram. *Albemarle* was designed with a shallow draft to operate in the rivers and sounds of North Carolina. Construction began in January 1863 under the supervision of nineteen-year-old Gilbert Elliott at Edward's Ferry, some sixty miles up the Roanoke from Plymouth. Commander James W.

Cooke was assigned to obtain railroad iron for the plating and to otherwise assist Elliott, eventually becoming the driving force behind the construction of the vessel. Difficulties in obtaining materials and equipment delayed completion until the spring of 1864. Like other Confederate ironclads beginning with the *Virginia*, *Albemarle* was built with a sloping casemate of heavy timbers and armored with iron plate. She carried two powerful Brooke rifles on pivots fore and aft, with gun ports allowing fire on either beam as well as forward and astern. The effectiveness of this design was, however, somewhat obviated by the time and manpower required to pivot the rifles into the desired position in the heat of battle. In addition to the guns, *Albemarle* sported a heavily reinforced and armor-plated bow to employ as a ram. Union authorities in North Carolina soon became aware of the construction of the ironclad and petitioned the War Department for an expedition overland to destroy the ship while still on the stocks. However, nothing effective was done. On April 18, 1864, under the command of Cooke, *Albemarle* steamed downstream to cooperate with the Confederate army in an attack on Plymouth. Early on April 19, Cooke engaged the small Union squadron at Plymouth. The Union commander, Lieutenant Commander Charles W. Flusser, had formulated a plan to trap the ironclad between his two largest vessels, the double-ender gunboats *Southfield* and *Miami*, which had been chained at the stern. However, Cooke sheered, ramming the *Southfield*, which immediately began to sink, dragging the *Albemarle* down with her. Flusser was killed by a ricocheting shell from a cannon he personally fired from the *Miami*. The *Southfield* settled on the bottom, allowing the *Albemarle* to pull free. The *Miami* and the smaller units of the squadron retreated downriver. Besieged by Confederate land forces and under fire from the *Albemarle*, the Union garrison ashore surrendered the next day. The fall of Plymouth was a serious blow to Union control of the North Carolina sounds. No available Union ironclad was of sufficiently shallow draft to pass over the bar from the ocean, forcing the navy to prepare for battle against the *Albemarle* with its wooden vessels. On May 5, *Albemarle* steamed into Albemarle Sound with the steamer *Cotton Planter* and the small gunboat *Bombshell*. Captain Melancton Smith steamed to intercept with the double-enders *Sassacus*, *Miami*, *Mattabesett*, and *Wyalusing* and three smaller gunboats. The *Cotton Planter* steamed back up the Roanoke. The *Bombshell* soon surrendered, but the Union gunboats were unable to do significant damage to the *Albemarle* in two and a half hours of close-quarters fighting. The *Sassacus* rammed the ironclad without effect and was herself seriously damaged by a shell from one of the *Albemarle*'s Brooke rifles. The action broke off about 7:30 P.M., the *Albemarle*, the draft of her furnaces reduced by damage to her smokestack, limped back to Plymouth. On June 17, 1864, Cooke was relieved by Commander John Newland Maffitt, who hoped to employ the *Albemarle* aggressively. However, Confederate authorities were unwilling to risk the ironclad so long as its presence alone prevented further attempts by Union forces to regain full control of the sounds. Lieutenant Alexander F. Warley relieved Maffitt on September 10, 1864, and was in command of the *Albemarle* at the time of Cushing's raid on the night of October 27, 1864. Following the sinking of the *Albemarle*, Union forces quickly recaptured Plymouth. Raised on March 18, 1865, the ironclad was lightened by stripping away most of her armor so that repairs could be made more easily to her hull. She was towed to Norfolk, arriving on April 27, where she was purchased by the navy from the prize court for $79,944. With the war nearly over, the Navy Department had no interest in repairing and re-armoring her, and she languished at an out-of-the-way pier, her hull rapidly deteriorating, until sold for salvage in 1867. Today, a sixty-three-foot replica of the *Albemarle* floats off the Plymouth waterfront not far from the naval museum. Displacement: 376 tons. Length: 158'. Beam: 35'. Draft: 8' 2''. Armament: ironclad ram and two 8-inch Brooke pivot rifles.

Alexander Cooper

Sloop destroyed by Cushing and a boat party from *Shokokon* in New Topsail Inlet, August 22, 1863.

Cambridge

Steamer built in Medford, Massachusetts, in 1860. She was purchased by the navy and commissioned August 29, 1861. Cushing "did midshipman's duty" aboard the *Cambridge* from October 1861 until March 1862, seeing "sharp action" on the Rappahannock and James rivers. *Cambridge* continued to serve in the North Atlantic Blockading Squadron until late in the war when she was reassigned to the South Atlantic Blockading Squadron. In total she took or destroyed eleven vessels. She was decommissioned in Philadelphia and sold June 20, 1865. Displacement: 868 tons. Length: 200'. Beam: 32'. Draft: 13' 6''. Speed: 10 knots. Complement: 96. Armament: two 8-inch rifles.

Charlotte

Large blockade-running steamer captured by Cushing and a boarding party at Smithville on January 20, 1865, interrupting the captain's dinner with his passengers, including several British army officers.

Chickamauga

(Cushing spelled it *Chickamaugua*.) Screw steamer. Built as the block-ade-runner *Edith* in London in 1863, she was purchased by the Confederate government and converted into a commerce raider at Wilmington, North Carolina. She took several prizes in a cruise in the western North Atlantic in October–November 1864. Employed in the defense of Wilmington and Fort Fisher, the *Chickamauga* was challenged by Cushing and the *Monticello* in late December 1864 but, much to Cushing's disgust, refused to abandon the shelter of Fort Caswell's guns. On January 15, 1865, during the bombardment of Fort Fisher by the Union fleet, Cushing drove off the *Chickamauga* and several smaller vessels from an attempt to reinforce the fort. Her crew burned *Chickamauga* on February 25, 1865, in the Cape Fear River to avoid capture. Displacement: 585 tons. Complement: 120. Armament: three rifled guns.

Coeur de Lion

(Cushing spelled the name *Coeur de Leo*.) A side-wheel steamer loaned to the navy by the Lighthouse Board, she was refitted and entered service on October 2, 1861. Patrolling the Potomac, James, Appomattox, Nansemond, and other rivers in Virginia and North Carolina, *Coeur de Lion* captured or de-stroyed eight vessels and supported amphibious operations. She was decommis-sioned June 2, 1865, and returned to the Lighthouse Board. Displacement: 110 tons. Length: 100'. Beam: 20'. Draft: 4' 6". Complement: 29. Armament: one 12-pounder rifle; one 12-pounder smoothbore; one 30-pounder smoothbore.

Cohasset

Tug built in Providence, Rhode Island, and christened *E. D. Fogg*. Sub-sequently, she was rechristened *Narragansett*. Purchased by the navy on Sep-tember 13, 1861, she served as a picket and dispatch boat, as well as a tug. *Cohasset* saw action on the York, James, and Nansemond Rivers. Postwar, she served as a yard tug in Boston and Newport, Rhode Island, until sold May 9, 1892. Displacement: 100 tons. Length: 82'. Beam: 19'. Speed: 8 knots. Complement: 12. Armament: one 20-pounder rifle.

Colorado

Screw frigate commissioned May 12, 1858, at Norfolk Navy Yard. She was active in the Gulf Blockading Squadron from June 1861 to February 1864. (Cushing was briefly aboard while *Colorado* was en route from New York via the Charleston blockading station.) Following overhaul at Norfolk, she joined the North Atlantic Blockading Squadron in October 1864, participating in the bombardment of Fort Fisher in January 1865, being struck six times. She continued in active service until 1875, after which she was a receiving ship at New York Navy Yard until sold February 14, 1885. Displacement: 4,772 tons. Length: 263' 8". Beam: 51' 4". Draft: 26' 2". Speed: 9 knots under steam. Complement: 646. Armament: two 10-inch pivot rifles; twenty-four 9-inch Dahlgren smoothbores; fourteen 8-inch Dahlgren smoothbores.

Commodore Barney

Side-wheel ferry built in 1859 at New York as the *Ethan Allen*. She was purchased by the navy October 2, 1861, and named for Joshua Barney (1759–1818), a naval hero of the Revolution and the War of 1812. She served actively in Virginia and North Carolina waters as part of the North Atlantic Blockading Squadron, participating in the capture of Roanoke Island and New Bern. Cushing commanded her from late January to late July 1863. She was decommissioned at Washington Navy Yard and sold July 20, 1865. Displacement: 512 tons. Length: 143'. Beam: 33'. Draft: 9'. Speed: 8 knots. Complement: 96. Armament: one 100-pounder Parrot rifle; five 100-pounder smoothbores; one 12-pounder howitzer.

Commodore Perry

Side-wheel ferry built in 1859 at Williamsburg, New York. She was purchased by the navy October 2, 1861, and named for War of 1812 naval hero Commodore Oliver Hazard Perry (1785–1819) and his brother, Matthew Calbraith Perry (1794–1858), the distinguished officer who "opened Japan." She saw extremely active service in the North Atlantic Blockading Squadron in Virginia and North Carolina waters, including the capture of Roanoke Island, Elizabeth City, and New Bern. Cushing requested duty aboard so he could serve under his friend and former instructor, Lieutenant Commander Charles W. Flusser. His request was approved, and he became the *Commodore Perry*'s executive officer in July 1862. On October 3, Flusser took *Commodore Perry*, *Whitehead*, and *Hunchback* up the Blackwater River to support an army expedition against Franklin, Virginia. (Unbeknownst to Flusser, the expedition had been delayed.) Encountering heavy fire from the shore, the ships had to fight their way downriver. Cushing distinguished himself by repelling an attempted boarding with a blast of canister from the deck howitzer. Reporting on the action, Flusser recommended that Cushing be given his own ship. Soon after, Cushing was detached from the *Commodore Perry* to take command of the *Ellis*. The *Commodore Perry* was decommissioned June 26, 1865, at New York City and sold July 12, 1865. Displacement: 512 tons. Length: 143'. Beam: 33'. Draft: 10'. Speed 7 knots. Complement: 125. Armament: two 9-inch rifles; two 32-pounder smoothbores; one 12-pounder howitzer.

Congress

Sail frigate. The fourth naval ship to bear the title, *Congress* was launched at the Navy Yard at Portsmouth, New Hampshire, August 16, 1841. She saw active duty in the South Atlantic and the Pacific. During the Mexican War, detachments from her crew fought ashore in the capture of southern California. *Congress* bombarded Guaymas, Mexico, and a detachment occupied Mazatlan in the fall of 1847. Subsequently, *Congress* served in the Mediterranean, in the interdiction of the African slave trade, and in the Brazil squadron. Returning from the latter shortly after the outbreak of the Civil War, *Congress* was attached to the Atlantic Blockading Squadron. Anchored off Newport News in Hampton Roads, Virginia, she was attacked on March 8, 1862, by the CSS *Virginia* (the former USS *Merrimack*). After suffering heavy casualties and unable to respond effectively against the ironclad, *Congress* struck her colors. Shore battery fire drove off the Confederate prize party, whereupon *Virginia* fired hot shot to set the vessel ablaze. *Congress* burned throughout the evening, a pyre to her brave crew and the age of fighting sail, exploding about midnight. The hulk was raised in September 1865 and sold. Displacement: 1,867 tons. Length: 179'. Beam: 47' 10". Draft: 22'. Complement: 480. Armament: four 8-inch rifles; forty-eight 32-pounder smoothbores.

Cumberland

Sail frigate/sloop. Built as a frigate, *Cumberland* was launched May 24, 1842, at Boston Navy Yard. She saw active duty antebellum, serving in the Mediterranean, African, and Home Squadrons and in the Gulf of Mexico during the Mexican War. In 1856, she was razeed (cut down) and made into a sail sloop, her lower profile making it possible for her to carry heavy Dahlgren shell guns. At Norfolk Navy Yard at the outbreak of the Civil War, she was towed to safety. Assigned to the North Atlantic Blockading Squadron, she was at anchor off Newport News in Hampton Roads on March 8, 1862, when she was attacked by the CSS *Virginia* (nee *Merrimack*). Although armed with powerful guns, she was unable to damage the ironclad significantly. Holed by the *Virginia*'s ram, *Cumberland* sank with her flag flying, her guns in action until the last. Since 1981, the *Cumberland*'s wreck, which lies near that of the CSS *Florida*, has been studied extensively by marine archaeologists. Original displacement: 1,726 tons. Length: 175'. Beam: 45'. Draft: 21'. Complement: 400. Armament (at the time of the battle of Hampton Roads): one 70-pounder pivot rifle; one 10-inch Dahlgren pivot smoothbore; twenty-two 9-inch Dahlgren smoothbores.

Delaware Farmer

A schooner captured by the *Minnesota* and sailed from Hampton Roads to Philadelphia by Cushing as prize master in May 1861.

Ellis

Iron-hulled side-wheel steamer. She was purchased at Norfolk in 1861 by the government of North Carolina and turned over to the Confederate navy at the time of the state's secession. She was captured by Union forces at the battle of Elizabeth City, North Carolina, on February 10, 1862, while under the command of James W. Cooke, the Confederate officer who would later command the *Albemarle*. Attached to the North Atlantic Blockading Squadron, *Ellis* patrolled the rivers and sounds of North Carolina. Cushing assumed command—his first—in October 1862. In a raid up New River, the *Ellis* grounded on the return trip. Unable to refloat his ship, Cushing set the *Ellis* ablaze on November 25, 1862, her 32-pounder loaded so that it would deliver a final defiant shot when the flames reached the gun. Displacement: 100 tons. Draft: 6'. Complement: 28. Armament: one 32-pounder rifle; one 12-pounder howitzer.

Harriet Lane

Side-wheel steamer. Named for the niece and official hostess of the bachelor president James Buchanan, the *Harriet Lane* had an extraordinarily active career. Built as a revenue cutter in New York City, she was launched in November 1857. She was transferred to the navy in late 1858 as part of a naval show of force in Paraguay, which had refused to settle a claim for an unprovoked attack on an American ship in 1855. Flag officer W. B. Shubrick, commanding the expedition, praised the vessel for repeatedly extricating deeper draft ships that had run aground in the shallow Parana River. Returned to the revenue service, *Harriet Lane* was put at the service of Edward Albert, Prince of Wales, during his visit to America. Transferred again to the navy on March 30, 1861, the *Harriet Lane* participated in the failed attempt to relieve Fort Sumter as hostilities began. The vessel sailed with the expedition that captured Forts Hatteras and Clark and opened the North Carolina sounds to the Union navy in August 1861. During Farragut's campaign to capture New Orleans in the spring of 1862, she served as Commodore David D. Porter's flagship while his mortar boats bombarded Forts Jackson and St. Phillip. That summer she shepherded the mortar boats upstream in Farragut's attempt on *Vicksburg*. On October 3, 1862, she led the expedition to capture Galveston. However, the Confederates retook the port on January 1, 1863, capturing the *Harriet Lane* after a fierce fight. Sold to a private citizen, she was converted into a blockade-runner and renamed *Lavinia*. Interned at Havana, she was returned to American ownership after the war. Converted to a bark rig and renamed the *Elliot Richie*, she was abandoned off Pernambuco, Brazil, May 13, 1884. Displacement: 600 tons. Armament: two 32-pounder smoothbores.

Hebe

Described by Cushing as a "large blockade-runner," she was driven ashore on Federal Point (Confederate Point) at the mouth of the Cape Fear River by the blockader *Niphon* on August 18, 1863. Cushing and *Shokokon* came to the assistance of *Niphon* when her boarding party was stranded aboard the *Hebe* by rough seas and a wrecked boat. Unable to rescue the boarding party, *Shokokon* joined the *Niphon* in setting the *Hebe* ablaze with shellfire after the Union sailors surrendered to Confederate cavalry on the beach.

Hetzel

Side-wheel steamer. Built in 1861 at Baltimore for the U.S. Coast Survey, she was transferred to the navy August 21, 1861, and assigned to the Atlantic Blockading Squadron. With other Union gunboats, she engaged the CSS *Patrick Henry* on December 2, 1861, at Hampton Roads. She participated in the Union capture of Roanoke Island February 5–8, 1862, and the defeat of the "mosquito fleet" at Elizabeth City on February 10. She also took part in the attack on New Bern, March 13–14, 1862. On patrol in the sounds and rivers of North Carolina, she participated in numerous actions. Until 1864, she was under the command of Commander Henry Davenport, the senior officer in the sounds, and hence served as flagship. She was returned to the Coast Survey in October 1865. Displacement: 200 tons. Armament: one 9-inch smoothbore; one 80-pounder smoothbore.

Hope

Forty-ton, centerboard schooner captured by Cushing at New River and used to escape the grounded *Ellis* on November 25, 1862, and again in his raid up Little River in February 1863. A fast blockade-runner also named *Hope* operated on the coast.

Hunchback

A side-wheel ferryboat built in 1852 at New York City and purchased by the navy December 16, 1861. She participated in the capture of Roanoke Island in February 1862 and the capture of New Bern in March. She patrolled the rivers and sounds of North Carolina, participating in the sharp engagement on the Blackwater River on October 3 in which Cushing distinguished himself as executive officer of the *Commodore Perry*. Decommissioned at New York June 12, 1865. Sold in 1866, she remained in civilian service until 1880. Displacement: 517 tons. Length 179'. Beam 29'. Speed: 12 knots. Armament: three 9-inch smoothbores; one 100-pounder Parrot rifle.

Malvern

Side-wheel steamer. Built in 1860 at Wilmington, Delaware, as the *William A Hewes*, she commenced service as a passenger packet between New York City and New Orleans in January 1861. She was seized April 28 by the government of Louisiana and employed as a blockade-runner under the name *Ella and Annie*. Large and fast, she was a notable success. She transferred her operations to Charleston after the fall of New Orleans in April 1862. She was captured by the *Niphon* on November 9, 1863, while attempting to enter Wilmington, North Carolina. Converted to a warship, she was commissioned as *Malvern* in February 1864 and assigned to the North Atlantic Blockading Squadron. Cushing commanded her December 2–27, 1864, during the first assault on Fort Fisher. Late in the war, she operated in the James River area. A luxurious ship, she was a favorite for the military conferences of Grant, Lincoln, and Admiral Porter. She participated in the capture of Fort Fisher in January 1865. On April 2, 1865, she conveyed Lincoln to Richmond after the fall of the Confederate capital. Restored to civilian service in October 1865, she was in operation under her original name until wrecked off the Cuban coast February 20, 1895. Displacement: 1,477 tons. Length: 239' 4". Beam: 33'. Draft: 10'. Armament: four 20-pounder Dahlgren rifles; eight 12-pounder smoothbores.

Maumee

Kansas-class sloop-rigged gunboat, a design intended to improve on the famous ninety-day gunboats. Built at the New York Navy Yard and commissioned September 29, 1864. She joined the North Atlantic Blockading Squadron, cruising in search of the Confederate raider *Tallahassee* and then participated in the attacks on Fort Fisher in December 1864 and January 1865. Joining the James River Squadron, she was one of the ships assigned to occupying the Richmond waterfront after the fall of the Confederate capital. Following an overhaul at Philadelphia, she was assigned to Cushing in October 1867 for a cruise of the Far East. As a part of the Asiatic Squadron, she chased pirates and otherwise protected American trading interests. She was sold at auction in Hong Kong December 15, 1869. *Yantic*, one of her sisters, remained in service in various capacities until 1929. Displacement: 593 tons. Length: 190'. Beam: 29'. Draft: 11'3". Speed: 11.5 knots. Complement: 96. Armament: one 100-pounder Parrot rifle; one 30-pounder Parrot rifle; one 12-pounder rifle; four 24-pounder smoothbores.

Merrimack

Screw frigate. The Merrimack was named after the Merrimack River, not the town of Merrimac, Massachusetts, and was carried on navy rolls under that spelling. After her conversion to the CSS *Virginia*, she continued to be referred to by her original name in popular usage but frequently without the terminal *k*. Built at Boston and commissioned February 20, 1856, *Merrimack* was one of the most modern and formidable ships in the navy. She made her maiden voyage to the Mediterranean, returned to Boston for repairs, and departed October 17, 1857, bound round the Horn for two years as flagship of the Pacific Squadron. On her return, her balky engines necessitated an extensive overhaul at Gosport Navy Shipyard in Hampton Roads. Anticipating the onset of hostilities, Secretary of the Navy Welles directed the transfer of the *Merrimack* to Philadelphia the day before the bombardment of Fort Sumter. However, she was still at Gosport, her engines partially disassembled, when Confederate sympathizers sank obstructions in the channel between Craney Island and Sewell's point on the night of June 16, 1861, blocking *Merrimack*'s departure. Virginia seceded the next day. Desperate to keep as much matériel as possible from falling into rebel hands, navy personnel burned the *Merrimack* and much of the yard on June 20, 1861. Following a proposal by Lieutenant J. M. Brooke, CSN, the hull was raised and an armored casemate built atop it. The resulting ironclad CSS *Virginia* was tremendously powerful, but retained many of the original *Merrimack*'s liabilities, particularly deep draft and cranky engines. Despite Northern fears, her draft and poor seaworthiness made her incapable of operations outside of the sheltered waters of Hampton Roads. Commissioned February 17, 1862, she steamed into the Roads on March 8, 1862, attacking and destroying the *Cumberland* and *Congress*, before the receding tide forced her return to the shelter of the south side of the Roads. The following day she met the *Monitor* in the famous drawn battle that would usher in a new era in sea warfare. She never fought again, although her presence continued to bedevil the Union fleet until Norfolk was taken by Union land forces in May. Unable to lighten the vessel sufficiently to escape up the James River to Richmond, her crew burned her on May 11, 1862. Her design was reproduced in nearly all the Confederate ironclads built during the war. Original displacement: 4,635 tons. Length: 256' 10". Beam: 50' 2". Draft: 26' 2". Speed: 9 knots under steam. Complement: 646. Armament: two 10-inch pivot rifles; twenty-four 9-inch Dahlgren smoothbores, fourteen 8-inch Dahlgren smoothbores. Ironclad (*Virginia*) displacement: 4,200 tons. Draft: 22'. Speed: 6 knots. Complement: 330. Armament: two 7-inch Brooke pivot rifles; two 6-inch Brooke rifles; six 9-inch smoothbores.

Minnesota

Screw frigate. Built at Washington Navy Yard and commissioned on May 21, 1857, *Minnesota* spent her antebellum service in the Orient with the East India Squadron. She became flagship of the Atlantic Blockading Squadron in May 1861, capturing or destroying several prizes, including the *Delaware Farmer*, which Cushing sailed to Philadelphia as prize master. In August 1861, *Minnesota* led the expedition that captured Hatteras Inlet, North Carolina. On March 8, 1862, the first day of the Battle of Hampton Roads, *Minnesota* grounded while trying to go to the aid of *Congress* and *Cumberland*, then under attack by the *Virginia/Merrimack*. Having finished off the *Congress* and *Cumberland*, the Confederate ironclad turned on the *Minnesota* but was unable to close because of fear that she, too, would go aground. Still, her guns inflicted significant damage at long range, while *Minnesota*'s had no impact at all. When *Monitor* arrived that night, she was ordered to protect *Minnesota* from the *Virginia*. These orders somewhat restricted the movements of the *Monitor* and discouraged her from pursuing the *Virginia* at the end of the four-hour drawn battle on March 9, 1862. *Minnesota* served throughout the remainder of the war in the North Atlantic Blockading Squadron. Although her slow speed made her ineffective against the speedy blockade-runners of the later years of the war, she used her heavy guns to good effect in the bombardment of Fort Fisher in December 1864 and January 1865. Two hundred forty of her crew joined the bloody land assault on the fort on January 15, 1865. She remained on the navy's roles until 1898 as a training ship. She was sold and burned on the beach at Eastport, Maine, in 1901 to recover her metal fittings. Displacement: 4,833 tons. Length: 264' 8". Beam: 50' 2". Draft: 26' 2". Speed: 9 knots under steam. Complement: 646. Armament: two 10-inch pivot rifles; twenty-four 9-inch Dahlgren smoothbores; fourteen 8-inch Dahlgren smoothbores.

Monitor

Ironclad. Without question the most famous Union warship of the Civil War, *Monitor* was built in four months after the awarding of her contract to John Ericsson on October 4, 1861. Commissioned on February 25, 1862, under the command of Lieutenant John Worden, she sailed under tow for

Hampton Roads on March 6, 1862. She arrived in the Roads in the late afternoon of March 8 to find the Union fleet devastated by the attack of the Confederate ironclad *Virginia* (the former *Merrimack*). On March 9 *Monitor* and *Virginia* fought a four-hour drawn engagement that would go down as one of the most famous naval battles in history. Cushing was a witness. *Monitor* foundered under tow on the night of December 30–31, 1862, while under tow off Cape Hatteras en route to Beaufort, North Carolina. Her wreck was discovered in August 1973. Too fragile to bring to the surface intact, various pieces have been raised in recent years. The site is now a National Marine Sanctuary. The turret, engines, and a full-scale replica are housed at the USS *Monitor* Center at the Mariners' Museum in Newport News, Virginia. Displacement: 987 tons. Length: 172'. Beam: 41' 6". Draft: 10' 6". Speed: 7–8 knots. Complement: 47. Armament: two 11-inch Dahlgren smoothbores.

Monticello
   Screw steamer built in Mystic, Connecticut, in 1859. Purchased by the navy September 12, 1861, she commenced her extremely active service as part of the James River Squadron. On May 10, 1861, she exchanged fire with a Confederate battery on Sewell's Point, suffering several casualties in what some sources, including Cushing himself, considered the first naval engagement of the war. Attached to the North Atlantic Blockading Squadron, *Monticello* patrolled the sounds and rivers of North Carolina, participating in numerous actions. Cushing commanded her from September 5, 1863, to mid-July 1864, when he was detached to prepare for the attack on the *Albemarle*. In the meantime, he had performed several of the raids described in his memoir. The sinking of the *Albemarle* won Cushing command of the flagship *Malvern*. However, he was unhappy with the duty, and Admiral Porter returned him to command of the *Monticello*, Cushing's favorite ship, on December 27, 1864. Cushing handed over the command on February 24, 1865, to go on leave. *Monticello* was decommissioned on July 24, 1865, at Portsmouth, New Hampshire, and sold at auction at Boston November 1, 1865. She foundered off Newfoundland April 29, 1872. Displacement: 655 tons. Length: 180'. Beam: 29'. Draft: 12' 10". Speed: 11.5 knots. Complement: 96. Armament: one 9-inch smoothbore; two 32-pounder smoothbores.

Mount Washington
   Side-wheel steamer built at Philadelphia in 1846, she operated in commercial service as the *Mount Vernon*. She was acquired by the navy in April 1861 and placed in commission under her original name. The name was changed to *Mount Washington* in November to prevent confusion with

another *Mount Vernon*. She was employed in Virginia and North Carolina waters in a number of capacities, including gunboat. She accompanied Cushing (in the *Commodore Barney*) on an expedition up the Nansemond River in April 1863, sustaining heavy damage from Confederate cannon ashore. Decommissioned and sold in June 1865. Broken up in 1885. Displacement: 646 tons. Armament: at least one 32-pounder smoothbore, otherwise unrecorded.

Nashville

Side-wheel steamer built at New York in 1853. Running between New York and Charleston, she was seized by Confederate authorities following the fall of Fort Sumter. Made into a commerce raider, she was the first vessel to fly the Confederate flag. On her initial cruise between October 21, 1861, and February 28, 1862, she captured two prizes. In March 1862 she was briefly blockaded at Beaufort, North Carolina, by the *Cambridge*, on which Cushing was serving. After escaping Beaufort and arriving in Charleston, she was sold to private parties and renamed the *Thomas L. Wragg* and employed in blockade running. Trapped in the Ogeechee River, Georgia, in June, she was closely blockaded by Union ships out of fear that she would be turned into an ironclad. On November 5, 1862, she was rechristened as the privateer *Rattlesnake*. After several attempts to escape, she grounded hard on February 27, 1863, and was destroyed the next day by the Union monitor *Montauk*. Her wreck is the subject of ongoing marine archaeology. Displacement: 1,221 tons. Length: 215' 6". Beam: 34' 6". Draft: 21' 9". Speed: 13 knots. Complement: 40. Armament: two 12-pounder smoothbores. A second *Nashville*, this one an ironclad ram, was constructed at Montgomery, Alabama, and towed to Mobile. Never completed, she was surrendered by Confederate authorities at Nana Hubba, Alabama, on May 10, 1865.

Pawnee

Screw sloop. One of the most active and successful Union ships of the Civil War, *Pawnee* was built at Philadelphia Navy Yard and commissioned June 11, 1860. In April 1861, she sailed for Charleston as part of the expedition to relieve Fort Sumter but arrived too late. Ordered to Hampton Roads, she participated in the burning of Gosport Navy Yard and towed the sloop *Cumberland* to safety on April 20. She cruised the Potomac in May, convoying ships and engaging shore batteries, before joining the Atlantic Blockading Squadron. She joined the expeditions to open Hatteras Inlet, North Carolina, in August and Port Royal Sound, South Carolina, in October 1861. Transferred to the South Atlantic Blockading Squadron, *Pawnee* cruised in South Carolina, Georgia, and Florida waters for the rest of the war except for a refit in Philadelphia in the fall of 1862. Her distinguished record included the capture of a number of blockade-runners and the conducting of numerous amphibious operations. In 1869, *Pawnee*'s engines were removed and she was converted into a sailing vessel. Her cruising days done, she served as a hospital and store ship until decommissioned in 1882. She was sold in 1884. Displacement: 1,533 tons. Length: 221' 6". Beam: 47'. Draft: 10'. Speed: 10 knots. Complement: 181. Armament (original): four 11-inch pivot smoothbores. Overhauled armament: twelve 9-inch smoothbores; two "large rifles"; two 12-pounder smoothbore howitzers (the latter probably present in both configurations).

Peterhoff

Side-wheel steamer. A British blockade-runner, she was captured by the *Vanderbilt* on February 25, 1863. A dispute about the legality of the capture delayed purchase from the prize court by the navy until February 1864. Assigned to the North Atlantic Blockading Squadron on February 20, 1864, *Peterhoff* was accidentally rammed and sunk on March 6, 1864, by the *Monticello* under the command of Cushing. Length: 210'. Beam: 28'. Displacement, complement, and armament unrecorded.

Pioneer

A bark captured by the *Minnesota* and sailed by Cushing as prize master from Hampton Roads to New York in the late spring of 1861.

Primrose

Screw tug. Originally the *Nellie B. Vaughn*, she was purchased by the navy January 14, 1863. Assigned to the Potomac Flotilla, *Primrose* often operated on the North Carolina sounds and rivers. She captured two prizes. After the war she served in the Washington Navy Yard until sold March 17, 1871. Displacement: 94 tons. Length: 83'. Beam: app. 18'. Draft: 7'. Complement: app. 12. Armament: one 30-pounder Parrot rifle; one 24-pounder howitzer.

Quaker City

Side-wheel steamer built at Philadelphia in 1854. She was chartered by the navy April 25, 1861, and purchased on August 12. Large and fast, she ranged widely in search of blockade-runners and commerce raiders, eventually capturing or destroying twenty-two vessels. She fought the Confederate ironclads *Chicora* and *Palmetto State* off Charleston on January 31, 1863. In December 1864 she participated in the first bombardment of Fort Fisher.

Decommissioned at Philadelphia, she was sold on June 20, 1865. She served in American commerce until sold abroad in 1869. Displacement: 1,600 tons. Length: 224' 8". Beam: 36'. Draft: 13' 8". Speed: 13 knots. Complement: 163. Armament: one 20-pounder Parrot rifle; eight 32-pounder smoothbores.

Raleigh

Ironclad built at Wilmington in 1863–1864. On May 6, 1864, she steamed out with consorts *Yadkin* and *Equator* and fought an inconclusive engagement against six Union blockaders. On the return run up the Cape Fear River, she struck Wilmington Bar and broke her back. She was still considered a threat until a party led by Cushing penetrated the river on June 25 and determined that the vessel was a complete wreck. In recent years, the *Raleigh*'s wreck has been the subject of archaeological study. Length: 150'. Beam: 32'. Draft: 12'. Complement: 188. Armament: four 6.4-inch Brooke rifles.

St. Lawrence

Sail frigate. Laid down in 1826, *St. Lawrence* was not completed until 1848. Antebellum, she conducted extended cruises in Northern European waters, the Mediterranean, the Pacific, and on the Brazil station, frequently serving as flagship. In the Civil War she served in the North Atlantic, South Atlantic, and East Gulf Blockading Squadrons. At Hampton Roads on March 8, 1862, she witnessed the *Virginia/Merrimack*'s attack on the *Cumberland* and *Congress*. Towed by the *Cambridge*, on which Cushing was serving, toward the scene, *St. Lawrence* ran aground. She exchanged fire with the Confederate ironclad at long range, suffering one hit. That night, she was towed to the safety of Fort Monroe. Following the war, she served for a decade as a barracks ship at Norfolk, where she was sold on December 31, 1875. Displacement: 1,726 tons. Length: 175'. Beam: 45'. Draft: 14' 5". Complement: 480. Armament: eight 8-inch smoothbores; forty-two 32-pounder smoothbores.

Sassacus

Side-wheel steamer. A classic double-ender, *Sassacus* was built at the Portsmouth (N.H.) Navy Yard and commissioned October 5, 1863, departing soon after for duty with the North Atlantic Blockading Squadron. Exceedingly fast and well armed, she destroyed two of the fastest English-built blockade-runners. On May 5, 1864, she was one of several Union ships to fight a furious battle with the Confederate ironclad *Albemarle* in Albemarle Sound. *Sassacus* rammed *Albemarle* broadside but was unable to inflict serious damage and was herself badly damaged by a shot from the ironclad. "Sadly yet honorably mutilated," she supported Grant's siege of Petersburg in the summer of 1864. Repaired in Philadelphia, she rejoined the fleet for the operations against Fort Fisher, December 1864–January 1865, and the subsequent campaign to capture Wilmington. Returning to Virginia waters, she supported army operations against Richmond. *Sassacus* was decommissioned May 13, 1865, at Philadelphia. She was sold August 28, 1868. Displacement: 974 tons. Length: 205'. Beam: 35'. Draft: 9'. Speed: 14.5 knots. Complement: 145. Armament: two 100-pounder Parrot rifles; one 12-pounder rifle; four 9-inch Dahlgren smoothbores; one 12-pounder smoothbore; two 24-pounder howitzers.

Shokokon (Shokoken)

(In his memoir, Cushing spelled the ship's name with an *–en*. Naval Records has the spelling as *–on*.) A wooden-hulled, side-wheel ferry built as *Clifton* in 1862 at Greenpoint, New York. She was purchased by the navy on April 3, 1863, and converted into a double-ender gunboat for service in Virginia and North Carolina waters. Cushing commanded the vessel August 9–September 5, 1863. He considered the ship "of doubtful seaworthiness" and was happy to leave her for command of the *Monticello*. Decommissioned at the New York Navy Yard, *Shokokon* was sold October 25, 1865, and recommissioned as *Lone Star*. She was abandoned in 1886. Displacement: 709 tons. Length: 181'. Beam: 32'. Draft: 13'. Speed: 10 knots. Complement: 112. Armament: two 30-pounder rifles; four 24-pounder smoothbores.

Southfield

Side-wheel ferry built in 1857 at Brooklyn and purchased by the navy on December 16, 1861. The double-ender gunboat joined the Atlantic Blockading Squadron and participated in the capture of Roanoke Island in early February 1862 as Admiral Goldsborough's flagship. She played a major role in the capture of Elizabeth City, New Bern, and Beaufort, North Carolina, in the succeeding weeks. Most of the summer she cruised the James and York Rivers in support of McClellan's Peninsular Campaign. On December 2 she was ordered to Plymouth, North Carolina, where she helped defend the strategic port from a Confederate attack on December 10. Disabled by a shot through the steam chest, she was towed to safety by the *Commodore Perry*. In the first two weeks of April 1863, she again helped repulse a Confederate attack on Plymouth. For the next year, she cruised the North Carolina sounds, using Plymouth as homeport much of the time. She engaged Confederate batteries on the Chowan River near New Bern on March 3, 1864. On April 19, 1864, *Southfield* and her consort *Miami* met the *Albemarle* at Plymouth, attempting to trap the Confederate ironclad between them. *Albemarle* sheered and rammed the *Southfield* on the starboard bow, tearing a huge hole in the hull and rupturing her boiler. Sinking, the *Southfield* nearly dragged the *Albemarle* down with her, but the ironclad managed to pull free while *Miami* and the other Union vessels fled. Plymouth surrendered the next day under bombardment from the *Albemarle* and the attack of the Confederate army. Displacement: 750 tons. Length: 200'. Beam: 34'. Draft: 6' 6". Speed: 12 knots. Complement: 61. Armament: one 100-pounder Parrot rifle; three 8-inch Dahlgren smoothbores.

Stag

Built as a Confederate blockade-runner at Liverpool, she departed for her maiden voyage in August 1864. She commenced the Nassau–Wilmington run in September, making several dashes through the blockade. Unaware of the fall of Fort Fisher on January 15, 1865, she was lured into the Cape Fear River on January 20 and captured by a boarding party led by Cushing. Sold to commercial interests, she was rechristened *Zenobia* and plied the New York–New Orleans run. In 1867, she was sold to Brazilian interests, remaining in service at least until 1885. Displacement: 600 tons. Length: 230'. Beam: 26'. Draft: 7' 6". Speed: 16 knots.

Stepping Stones

Side-wheel ferry built at New York City in 1861 and purchased by the navy on September 30. Fast and light draft, she saw busy service as a dispatch and patrol boat on the Potomac, James, York, and Rappahannock rivers. In April 1863, she participated in an operation on the Nansemond River under Cushing in the *Commodore Barney*. Late in the war she became part of the mine-clearing patrol on the James. Despite her light armament, she captured two prizes. Sold July 27, 1865, at Washington Navy Yard, she entered commercial service as *Cambridge*, one of several ships in commercial and naval service to bear the name. Eventually, her engines were removed and she was made into a barge. Displacement: 226 tons. Length: 100'. Beam: 24'. Draft: 4' 6". Speed: 14 knots. Complement: 21. Armament: one 12-pounder howitzer.

Stonewall

Brig-rigged, screw-driven, seagoing ironclad built in 1863–1864 by L'Arman shipyard in Bordeaux as the *Sphynx*. Protests by the United States ambassador and declining Confederate battlefield fortunes led the French government to forbid transfer of the vessel and three others building in France to Confederate ownership. *Sphynx* was sold to the Danish government as the *Staerkodder* for use in the Schleswig-Holstein war with Prussia.

However, the ironclad arrived at Copenhagen after peace had been concluded, and Denmark refused delivery after testing and finding her seaworthiness suspect. The French builder then sold her to the Confederate navy. Capt. Thomas J. Page, CSN, took command. (The names *Staerkodder* and *Olinde* were used to disguise her ownership.) On January 6, 1865, she steamed out of Copenhagen to rendezvous off the French coast with the *City of Richmond*, which carried the ship's armament and the rest of her crew. She was observed by shore spotters in the pay of the American ambassador, who sent a warning to Admiral Porter, commanding the North Atlantic Blockading Squadron. Porter put his ships on alert and dispatched Cushing to Norfolk in late February to mount a spar torpedo on the bow of the *Monticello*. In his memoir, Cushing referred to the threat of the "anglo-rebel ironclads," an understandable enough mistake after the years of controversy over the Laird rams. Rechristened *Stonewall*, the ironclad sailed for Madeira to complete provisioning but was forced into the Spanish port of Ferrol to fix a leak. The Federal cruisers *Niagara* and *Sacramento* intercepted her at Ferrol but refused combat when the *Stonewall* set to sea, a decision that would lead to the court-martial of the senior captain. After coaling in Lisbon, the *Stonewall* set off across the Atlantic, making landfall at Nassau on May 6, 1865. British authorities refused to allow the ironclad to enter port but permitted her to take on enough coal from a lighter to steam to Havana. Page and the *Stonewall*'s crew were kindly greeted at Havana, where Page was informed that the Confederacy had surrendered. In exchange for a loan to pay off his crew, Page presented the *Stonewall* as a gift to the queen of Spain. The Spanish turned over possession of the *Stonewall* to the United States in July 1866. She was subsequently sold to the shogun of Japan and renamed the *Kotetsu*. Arriving at Yokohama on April 24, 1868, she was seized by imperial forces at war with the shogun. In March 1869, she took a significant part in the invasion of Hokkaido and the battle of Hakodate against shogunate forces near the end of the Boshin War, which led to the Meiji Restoration. Cushing, in command of the *Maumee*, saw her in Edo Bay in late 1868 and graciously sent the captain some spare engine parts and rations. Renamed *Adzuma* in 1871, she remained in commission until 1888. She was broken up in 1908. Displacement: 1,358 tons. Length: 171' 10". Beam: 32' 8". Draft: 14' 4". Speed: 10 knots. Complement: 135. Armament: one 300-pounder Garnard rifle in forward turret; two 70-pounder Armstrong rifles in aft turret.

Susquehanna

Large side-wheel steamer built at New York Navy Yard and commissioned December 24, 1850. She sailed to the Far East, performing her most famous service as Commodore Matthew Perry's flagship during the opening of Japan in 1853. In 1856, she became flagship of the Mediterranean Squadron. Following a refit in New York in 1860, she returned to the Mediterranean, where news of the outbreak of the Civil War reached her. Arriving in Boston on June 6, 1861, she was assigned to the Atlantic Blockading Squadron. She participated in the capture of Hatteras Inlet in August 1861 and the capture of Port Royal and Beaufort in October and November 1861. She blockaded off Charleston until the spring of 1862, when she returned to Hampton Roads to support McClellan's Peninsular Campaign and the Union capture of Norfolk in May 1862. For the next year she served in Farragut's West Gulf Blockading Squadron before returning for a refit at New York Navy Yard on May 14, 1863. Rejoining the North Atlantic Blockading Squadron in July 1864, she participated in the operations against Fort Fisher, December 1864–January 1865. An effective blockader, she took or destroyed eight vessels. Decommissioned at New York Navy Yard on January 14, 1868, *Susquehanna* was laid up until sold for scrap September 27, 1883. Displacement: 2,450 tons. Length: 257'. Beam: 45'. Draft: 20' 6". Armament: two 150-pounder Parrot pivot rifles; twelve 9-inch Dahlgren smoothbores; one 12-pounder howitzer.

Valley City

Screw steamer built at Philadelphia in 1859 and purchased by the navy July 26, 1861. She saw duty in the Potomac Flotilla and was then assigned to the North Atlantic Blockading Squadron on January 4, 1862. She participated in the capture of Roanoke Island on February 7–8 and the battle of Elizabeth City against the "mosquito squadron." She performed active duty in the North Carolina sounds throughout the rest of the war, enforcing the blockade and participating in various amphibious operations. On October 28, 1864, she rescued the exhausted Cushing from the boat he'd stolen following his successful attack on the *Albemarle*. *Valley City* was decommissioned and sold August 15, 1865. She was lost at sea off Cape San Bias, Florida, on January 30, 1882. Displacement: 190 tons. Length: 127' 6". Beam: 21' 10". Draft: 8' 4". Speed: 10 knots. Armament: four 32-pounder smoothbores.

Vicksburg

Screw steamer built in 1863 at Mystic, Connecticut, and purchased by the navy on October 20, 1863. She performed picket duty off New York until ordered to the North Atlantic Blockading Squadron on February 8, 1864. She participated in the Fort Fisher campaign and then supported Grant's siege of Petersburg. She was decommissioned and sold at auction at New York August 7, 1865. Displacement: 886 tons. Length: 185'. Beam: 33'. Draft: 13' 8".

Speed: 9 knots. Armament: one 100-pounder Parrot rifle; four 30-pounder Parrot rifles, one 20-pounder Parrot rifle; one 20-pounder smoothbore. (The Confederate navy had another *Vicksburg*, a 635-ton side-wheel steamer, considered one of the largest and fastest vessels on the Mississippi. Employed in various capacities, she was damaged beyond effective repair by the *Queen of the West* at Vicksburg on February 2, 1863.)

Violet

Screw tug built at Brooklyn as the *Martha* in 1862 and purchased by the navy on December 30, 1862. Fast and seaworthy, *Violet* saw duty with the North Atlantic Blockading Squadron as both a tug and a blockader. A hard-luck vessel, she was nearly sunk in a storm off Cape Hatteras on her way to her first station. On December 20, 1863, she grounded while trying to tow off an abandoned blockade-runner and was almost lost a second time before her armament was heaved overboard and she could be got off. On August 7, 1864, she grounded on a shoal off Western Bar, North Carolina. Unable to free her, her crew set her ablaze to avoid capture. Cushing was offered command of the *Violet* or the *Commodore Barney* in January 1863, describing the former as "a fast boat intended for capture of prizes off Wilmington." He chose the *Commodore Barney* since "there was a good appearance of coming war about Norfolk." Displacement: 166 tons. Length: 85'. Beam: 19' 9". Draft: 11' 9". Armament: one 12-pounder rifle.

Virginia

Confederate steamer (as distinguished from the rebuilt USS *Merrimack*, rechristened CSS *Virginia* by the Confederates) that passed near Cushing's hidden men during their escape from the raid up the Cape Fear River in search of the ironclad *Raleigh* in June 1864.

Virginia (ironclad)

See *Merrimack*.

Wabash

Screw frigate. *Wabash* was built at the Philadelphia Navy Yard and commissioned in August 1856, becoming flagship of the home squadron. Assigned early in the Civil War to the Atlantic Blockading Squadron, she participated in the expeditions to capture Hatteras Inlet, North Carolina, and Port Royal, South Carolina, in the late summer and fall of 1861. Cushing was temporarily assigned to her in June–July 1861 at Charleston while waiting to rejoin the *Minnesota* after taking the bark *Pioneer* to New York as a prize. From 1862 to 1864, *Wabash* served as flagship of the South Atlantic Blockading Squadron. Too slow to chase blockade-runners and too deep draft for shallow waters, *Wabash* and her sisters were nevertheless powerful bombardment ships. She participated in the operations against Fort Fisher, North Carolina, in December 1864–January 1865 that resulted in the closing of Wilmington, the South's last major blockade-running port. Deactivated in February 1865, *Wabash* was restored to active service in 1871 and spent two years as flagship of the Mediterranean Squadron. From 1876 to 1912 she served as a receiving ship in Boston before being sold for scrap. Displacement: 4,774 tons. Length: 262' 4". Beam: 50' 2". Draft: 26' 2". Speed: 9 knots under steam. Complement: 646. Armament: two 10-inch pivot rifles; twenty-four 9-inch Dahlgren smoothbores; fourteen 8-inch Dahlgren smoothbores.

West End

Described by Cushing as "an army gunboat," she accompanied Cushing on a raid up the Nansemond River in April 1863.

Whitehead

Screw steamer built in 1861 at New Brunswick, New Jersey, and purchased by the navy on October 17, 1861. She was extremely active on the rivers and sounds of North Carolina, taking or destroying five vessels and supporting numerous shore operations. She clashed with the *Albemarle* on April 19, 1864, at the battle of Plymouth where Cushing's friend Lieutenant Commander Charles W. Flusser was killed. Retreating with other Union vessels to Albemarle Sound, *Whitehead* was a member of the squadron that fought *Albemarle* in a terrific two-hour fight on May 5. *Whitehead* and *Albemarle* again exchanged fire on May 24. On October 31, following Cushing's successful attack on the *Albemarle*, *Whitehead* participated in the recapture of Plymouth. Decommissioned at Philadelphia, she was sold on October 7, 1865. Renamed the *Nevada*, she was destroyed by fire on September 1, 1872, at New London, Connecticut. Displacement: 136 tons. Length: 93'. Beam: 19' 9". Draft: 8'. Speed: 8 knots. Armament: one 30-pounder Parrot rifle.

Wyoming

Screw sloop of war. Built at the Philadelphia Navy Yard and commissioned in October 1859, *Wyoming* was one of the long-lived *Mohican* class, the last of which served into the twentieth century. Built on an innovative design that put all the guns on pivots, the *Mohicans* could fire their entire batteries off either beam, giving the ships a tremendous amount of firepower with only six cannon. After a shakedown cruise, *Wyoming* was sent around the Horn. She would remain in Pacific waters to almost the end of the Civil War. For the first year of the war, she patrolled the west coasts of North and South America. In June 1862, she set sail for the Far East. She protected American trading interests and cruised for Confederate raiders. In the Sunda Strait between Java and Sumatra, she and the *Alabama* passed within twenty-five miles of each other, but it would fall to the *Wyoming*'s sister ship *Kearsarge* to finally meet and destroy the famous Confederate raider. In June 1863 an American merchant vessel, the *Pembroke*, was attacked in the Shimonoseki Strait south of Hiroshima by two ships flying the flag of the central government of Japan. The *Wyoming* went in search of the offending ships. On July 16, she sank one Japanese vessel and severely damaged two more, all the while engaging in a fierce duel with shore batteries. The action served to impress on the Japanese the determination of the United States to maintain trading rights. For the balance of her war service, the *Wyoming* continued to cruise for Confederate raiders. She returned to the United States for a badly needed overhaul, arriving at Philadelphia on July 13, 1864. She was back at sea almost immediately, searching for the Confederate raider *Florida*. She returned six days later and was decommissioned for her overhaul. In September 1865, she returned to the Far East to search for the Confederate raider *Shenandoah*, which was still carrying on raids against American ships months after the end of the war ashore. Returning to the United States in February 1868, she was decommissioned at Boston. After another extensive overhaul in 1870–1871, she was recommissioned. Cushing commanded her from July 1873 until April 1874, during which time the *Wyoming* intervened in the famous *Virginius* Incident in Santiago de Cuba. *Wyoming* continued in active service until 1882, when she became a practice ship for midshipmen at Annapolis. She was sold at that port on May 9, 1892. Displacement: 1,457 tons. Length: 198' 6". Beam: 33' 2". Draft: 14' 10". Speed: 11 knots. Complement: 198. Armament: two 11-inch Dahlgren smoothbores; three 32-pounder smoothbores; one 60-pounder Parrot rifle.

Yadkin

Confederate screw gunboat built at Wilmington in 1863–1864. Nominally the flagship of Commodore W. F. Lynch, she accompanied the ironclad *Raleigh* on its single engagement on May 6, 1864. She was sunk by the Confederates in mid-February 1865 to obstruct the Cape Fear River below Wilmington following the fall of Fort Fisher. Displacement: about 300 tons. Armament: one or two guns.

Yankee

Side-wheel tug, built in 1860 at New York City and chartered in April 1861 by the navy for the relief expedition to Fort Sumter. Arriving too late to help, *Yankee* sailed to Hampton Roads where she helped tow the *Cumberland* to safety during the evacuation of Gosport Navy Yard. She saw active service on the Potomac and James, capturing three prizes and supporting amphibious operations. At some point she was purchased by the navy. In April 1863 she joined the North Atlantic Blockading Squadron. On April 20, she participated in sharp fighting on the Nansemond River, the point at which Cushing refers to her in his memoir. *Yankee* continued to take an active part in operations on the rivers and sounds of North Carolina and Virginia until the end of the war. She was decommissioned and sold at New York City September 15, 1865. Displacement: 328 tons. Length: 146'. Beam: 25' 7''. Armament: two 32-pounder smoothbores.

Yorktown

Brig-rigged side-wheel steamer built in New York in 1859. A passenger steamer running between Richmond, Virginia, and New York, the ship was seized by Virginia authorities when the state seceded on April 17, 1861, and subsequently turned over to the Confederate navy. Rechristened *Patrick Henry*, she became part of the James River Squadron. Active against Union gunboats in Hampton Roads, she accompanied the *Virginia/Merrimack* in the famous battle on March 8–9, 1862, where she was observed by Cushing, who referred to her in his memoir by her original name. Moving to take the surrender of the *Congress* on the first day of the battle, she was driven off by Union shore batteries with the loss of four men. The action of the Union batteries so enraged the *Virginia/Merrimack*'s commander, Admiral Franklin Buchanan, that he ordered the Union vessel fired with hot shot. Following the surrender of Norfolk on May 10, 1862, the *Patrick Henry* retreated up the James with the rest of the small ships of the Confederate squadron to Drewry's Bluff. From then until April 1865, she served as the home of the Confederate Naval Academy at Richmond. She was burned to prevent capture during the evacuation of Richmond on April 3, 1865. Displacement: 1,300 tons. Length: 250'. Beam: 34'. Draft: 17'. Complement: 150. Armament: two 32-pounder rifles; six 8-inch rifles; one 64-pounder rifle; one 10-inch smoothbore.

APPENDIX 2

ᔥ

Officers Named in the Text

Abbreviations

CSA. Confederate States Army

CSN. Confederate States Navy

USMA. United States Military Academy (Class rank follows, e.g., 5/53, or fifth of fifty-three)

USMC. United States Marine Corps

USN. United States Navy

USNA. United States Naval Academy

USA. United States Army

USA(V). United States Army (volunteers)

Barron, Samuel

Commodore, CSN. 1809–1888. Born: Hampton, Virginia. Placed on the navy rolls at the age of two by his father, one of the heroes of the early navy, Barron entered active service as a midshipman at the age of eleven. He had an illustrious antebellum career, rising to the rank of captain. He tendered his resignation in April 1861 to join the Confederate navy. He organized coastal defenses in Virginia and North Carolina but lost the forts of Hatteras and Clark to the Stringham/Butler attack in August 1861. Captured, Barron was exchanged in 1862 for Lieutenant John L. Worden, who would win fame shortly after as captain of the *Monitor*. Barron commanded Confederate naval forces in Virginia until sent to Great Britain in November 1862 to oversee the building of commerce raiders and the famous Laird rams for the Confederacy. When Great Britain seized the Laird ironclads in 1863, Barron relocated to Paris, where he served as flag officer of Confederate naval forces in European waters until shortly before the defeat of the Confederacy. After the war, he retired to his farm in Essex County, Virginia.

Barton
Masters Mate on the *Ellis*.

Bragg, Braxton
General, CSA. 1817–1876. USMA 1837 (5/50). Born: Warrenton, North Carolina. Bragg served in the Seminole War and in posts in the East. He feuded frequently with his superiors, gaining a reputation as the "most disputatious officer in the army." A gifted artillery officer, Bragg performed superbly during Zachary Taylor's invasion of northern Mexico. At Buena Vista, Bragg's flying battery saved Jefferson Davis's regiment and probably the entire army. Bragg became a national hero after Taylor's famous order— "A little more grape, if you please, Captain Bragg"—was published in the press. (Taylor's actual wording was considerably saltier.) In 1856, Bragg left the army to become a planter. Considered among the best of the South's officers early in the war, he fought at Shiloh and then succeeded Beauregard in command of the Army of Tennessee. He excelled at training and discipline, but proved a poor combat commander: indecisive, inflexible, and hostile to subordinates. His invasion of Kentucky in the fall of 1862 failed miserably. His tactical inflexibility turned early success into a bloody stalemate in the battle of Stones River (Murfreesboro) at the turn of 1862–1863. The following summer he was maneuvered out of Middle Tennessee by William S. Rosecrans, evacuating Chattanooga in early September. Reinforced by two divisions under James Longstreet from the Army of Northern Virginia, Bragg struck Rosecrans at Chickamauga on September 19, winning—largely thanks to Longstreet's tactics—the largest battle in the West. However, he failed to follow up with a quick strike at Chattanooga, choosing instead to lay siege to the town and the demoralized Army of the Cumberland. George H. Thomas succeeded Rosecrans while Grant took overall command at Chattanooga. With powerful reinforcements from the Army of the Tennessee and the Army of the Potomac, Grant broke the siege in a three-day series of battles that climaxed with the Union assault and the Confederate rout at Missionary Ridge on November 25. Bragg resigned command of the Army of Tennessee, but his close friend Davis appointed him his military advisor. Bragg served in this capacity until dispatched to command the Cape Fear District (and three weeks later the newly formed Department of North Carolina) on October

22, 1864. He failed to adequately reinforce Fort Fisher, thereby dooming Wilmington, the Confederacy's last significant open port. Fort Fisher fell on January 16, 1865. Bragg evacuated Wilmington on February 21, 1865. He accompanied Davis on his flight into Georgia where he was captured on May 9, 1865, a day before the president. After the war he practiced engineering in Alabama and Texas, dying suddenly in Galveston on September 27, 1876. A gaunt, forbidding man with a malevolent stare, he was "the most hated man in the Confederacy," according to the diarist Mary Chesnut, an opinion largely unchallenged by subsequent generations.

Braine, Daniel Lawrence
Lieutenant Commander, USN. 1829–1898. Born: New York City. Appointed a midshipman in 1847, he served in the Mexican War. As captain of the gunboat *Monticello* he exchanged fire with the rebel battery on Sewell's Point in Hampton Roads on May 10–14, 1861, in what may have been—depending on definition—the first naval engagement of the Civil War. He participated in the capture of Hatteras Inlet in August 1861 and saw active service throughout the war. Postwar he commanded a search of Greenland waters for the lost Polaris Expedition to the arctic. He retired as a rear admiral.

Breese, Kidder R.
Lieutenant Commander, USN. 1831–1881. Born: Philadelphia. Appointed a midshipman in 1847, he served in the Mexican War. He took part in Commodore Matthew C. Perry's expedition to Japan 1852–1855. He served in the coastal survey and aboard various ships, including the *Preble* during its Paraguay expedition in 1858–1859. He was an officer aboard the *San Jacinto* during the famous Mason-Slidell incident. He commanded part of David Dixon Porter's mortar boat flotilla in Farragut's capture of New Orleans. He distinguished himself again during the siege of Vicksburg in the spring and summer of 1863 and became fleet captain when Porter assumed command of the North Atlantic Blockading Squadron in 1864. Breese led the doomed naval land assault on the northeastern bastion of Fort Fisher on January 15, 1865, suffering a bloody repulse that nevertheless distracted the Confederate defenders long enough for Union army troops to gain a foothold inside the fort's northwest corner. His postwar career was similarly distinguished and included a tour as commandant of the Naval Academy. Promoted to captain, he died in service.

Butler, Benjamin Franklin.
Major General, USA(V). 1818–1893. Born: New Hampshire. A Massachusetts militia general, noted lawyer, and influential Democratic politi-

cian, he was appointed to command of the District of Annapolis in early 1861. On his own initiative he occupied Baltimore on May 13, 1861, greatly easing the reinforcement of Washington, D.C., by Federal troops in the dire early days of the war. The first "political" major general appointed by the administration, he commanded Federal forces at Big Bethel Church, Virginia, on June 10, 1861, in what is often considered the first land battle of the war. Briefly in command at Fortress Monroe, he instituted the practice of designating escaped slaves as "contraband of war" and refusing to return them to their masters. Despite the defeat at Big Bethel Church, he was appointed to command the army force in the amphibious expedition that captured Forts Hatteras and Clark on Hatteras Inlet in August 1861. Although the success was almost entirely due to Commodore Silas Stringham's naval squadron, Butler claimed much of the credit as his own. After returning to Massachusetts to raise troops, he commanded the army supporting Farragut's expedition against New Orleans in the spring of 1862, where he again claimed more credit than his due. As military governor of the captured city, his high-handed treatment of local sentiments and his probable involvement in looting and graft soon earned him the nickname "Spoons" for allegedly amassing a large collection of looted silverware. This sardonic nickname was replaced by the obloquy "the Beast" after Butler threatened to treat any women who abused Federal troops as "women of the town," that is, prostitutes, and hanged a man who tore down the national banner. His seizure of Confederate bullion deposited at the Dutch consulate brought protests from abroad. Faced with a diplomatic embarrassment, the administration hastily replaced Butler with Major General Nathaniel P. Banks. Butler, still influential, was appointed to command the Department and Army of the James. In this capacity his military incompetence led to the bottling up of his army at Bermuda Hundred and his failure to capture Petersburg during Grant's 1864 overland campaign. In December 1865, he commanded Union land forces in the first attack on Fort Fisher. The failure of his famed "Powder Boat" on December 23 and his withdrawal of troops landed north of Fort Fisher in the days following the fiasco—a direct violation of Grant's orders—provided Grant with the ammunition to relieve Butler of further command. Postwar, Butler became a Radical Republican congressman and was among the leaders of the attempt to impeach President Andrew Johnson. Although frustrated in his ambitions to become president, Butler served a term as governor of Massachusetts and remained an influential politician until his death. Physically ugly, he took great pleasure in wearing uniforms loaded with gold braid.

Davenport, Henry K.

Commander, USN. 1820–1872. Born: Savannah, Georgia. Davenport entered the navy as a midshipman in 1838. He served in the Far East, the Mexican War, the Coast Survey, and the Naval Observatory. He commanded the gunboat *Hetzel* in the capture of Roanoke Island and New Bern. Through much of the war he was the senior officer in the North Carolina sounds, a position that gave him responsibility for all the ships and operations in one of the war's most challenging environments. He had frequent dealings with Cushing, usually but not always supporting his plans. Davenport was transferred to the Pacific Squadron late in the war. Promoted to captain, he commanded several vessels postwar, including the new *Congress* in the European Squadron. He died in service in 1872.

Dix, John Adams

Major General, USA(V). 1798–1879. Born: New Hampshire. Dix received a private education, entering army service at fourteen in 1812 as an ensign under the sponsorship of his father, a lieutenant colonel. Dix fought in the savage battle at Lundy's Lane, where both armies suffered losses of nearly a third. Dix continued in the army until 1828, when he resigned to practice law in upstate New York. As a Jackson Democrat, he held numerous county and state offices. He served in the United States Senate 1845–1849. For the next decade he practiced law and served as president of two railroads. Late in the Buchanan administration, he was appointed secretary of the Treasury. Commissioned a major general of volunteers by Lincoln, he was first on the seniority list. He commanded various departments throughout the war, proving a capable military administrator. He rushed troops to New York to suppress the draft riots (July 13–16, 1863). For the rest of the war, he commanded the Department of the East. He served as minister to France in the Johnson administration and subsequently a term as governor of New York.

Ellis

Lieutenant or Lieutenant Commander, USN. Referred to by Cushing as captain of the *Monticello* during the expedition to capture Hatteras Inlet in late August 1861. Otherwise unidentified.

Flusser, Charles W.

Lieutenant Commander, USN. 1832–1864. USNA 1853. Born: Maryland. While an instructor at Annapolis, Flusser became friends with Cushing. In the spring of 1861, the two spent several days together in Washington, during which time Flusser encouraged Cushing to seek reinstatement in the navy following the younger man's dismissal from the Naval Academy. Cushing, in turn, convinced Flusser to remain loyal to the Union. Ambitious and fearless, Flusser quickly gained a reputation in North Carolina waters as captain of a converted Staten Island ferry, the USS *Commodore Perry*. In the fight against the "mosquito fleet" at Elizabeth City on February 10, 1862, Flusser rammed and sank the Confederate flagship, *Sea Bird*. Cushing served under Flusser aboard the *Commodore Perry* July–October 1862. Flusser's commendation of Cushing's conduct at the fight on the Blackwater River secured Cushing his first command. Promoted to lieutenant commander, Flusser took charge of the gunboat squadron at Plymouth. When reports of the construction of the *Albemarle* reached Flusser, he prepared to grapple with the ironclad. On April 19, 1864, the *Albemarle*, commanded by Commander James W. Cooke, descended on Plymouth. Flusser met the ironclad with two double-ender gunboats, the *Southfield* and his flagship, the *Miami*, chained together at the stern in the hope of snagging the *Albemarle* between them. Cooke sheered at the last moment, ramming the *Southfield*. For a few moments, the *Southfield* and the *Albemarle* lay locked together. Flusser personally trained a nine-inch Dahlgren gun on the ironclad. The gun captain shouted a warning: "There's a shell in that gun, sir!" Flusser responded, "Never mind, my lad, we'll give them this first and solid shot after." But as the gunner had feared, the shell rebounded from the *Albemarle*'s plating and exploded over the gun crew, killing Flusser instantly. Without Flusser's gunboats to protect the town, Plymouth fell to the *Albemarle* and the Confederate army the next day, depriving the Union of a critical port for the control of Albemarle Sound. On hearing the news of Flusser's death, Cushing vowed revenge for the death of the friend he considered the *beau ideal* of a naval officer.

Foster, John Gray

Brigadier General, USA(V). USMA 1846 (4/59). 1823–1874. Born: New Hampshire. Graduating near the top of his class at West Point, Foster entered the prestigious Corps of Engineers. He won two brevets with Winfield Scott's army in Mexico. He spent the rest of his antebellum career teaching engineering at West Point and constructing various fortifications. He served at Fort Sumter during the bombardment by Confederate forces on April 12–14, 1861. Appointed a brigadier general of volunteers, he participated in Burnside's amphibious operations in the sounds of North Carolina. In July 1862, Foster became commander of the Department of North Carolina. In the fall of 1863, he participated in the relief of Burnside at Knoxville, succeeding him in command of the Army and Department of the Ohio. In

February 1865, he went on medical leave to recover from injuries sustained when a horse fell on him. He returned to his engineering duties after the war, serving until shortly before his death.

Fox, Gustavus Vasa

Captain, USN. Assistant Secretary of the Navy. 1821–1883. Born: Massachusetts. Appointed a midshipman in 1838, he served in various capacities and in the Mexican War. He resigned as a lieutenant in 1856 to manufacture woolens. Recalled to duty by General Winfield Scott in February 1861, he planned the relief of Fort Sumter but the expedition arrived only in time to evacuate the garrison. Lincoln created the post of assistant secretary of the Navy for Fox, who worked closely with Secretary of the Navy Gideon Welles. While Welles fought the department's political battles, Fox directed fleet operations. He oversaw the purchase of ships for the blockading fleet; championed Ericsson's *Monitor*; planned the expedition against New Orleans, arranging the appointment of Farragut to command; and directed the building of the ironclad gunboat fleet that played an instrumental role in opening the Mississippi. Officers in the navy universally acknowledged Fox's authority and ability as one of the principal architects of Union victory. As Secretary of State Seward's emissary in the Johnson administration, he negotiated the purchase of Alaska from Russia. He then returned to the woolens business. Historians have almost universally praised Fox for his drive, knowledge, and skills as an administrator. Some, however, have criticized his tendency to approve too many design changes in the building of the later classes of ironclads, slowing their completion and deployment. The failure of the shallow-draft ironclad program had a particular bearing on the naval war in the North Carolina sounds and rivers where the navy's oceangoing monitors could not enter, leaving the Union's wooden gunboats to battle Confederate land forces and ironclads at a considerable disadvantage.

Goldsborough, Louis M.

Rear Admiral, USN. 1805–1877. Born: Washington, D.C. Appointed a midshipman at seven, he began his active service in 1816. In 1827, he led a daring boat raid to rescue a British merchant ship from pirates. He proposed and then commanded the Depot of Charts and Instruments, later renamed the United States Hydrographic Office. He took leave to fight ashore in the Seminole War. He provided distinguished service in the Mexican War and later explored northern California and Oregon. He was superintendent of the Naval Academy 1853–1857. At the outbreak of the Civil War, he was commodore of the Brazil Squadron. He commanded the North Atlantic Blockading Squadron from October 1861 to September 1862, during which time he aided in Burnside's capture of Roanoke Island. Ordered to Washington, he undertook various administrative duties. He commanded the European Squadron in the last year of the war. From 1868 to his retirement in 1873, he commanded the Washington Navy Yard.

Gwin, William

Lieutenant, USN. 1832–1863. Born: Columbus, Indiana. Gwin entered the navy as a midshipman in 1832, seeing duty on several ships antebellum. He was promoted to lieutenant in 1855 and served in the Mediterranean and Pacific Squadrons (he had previously served in the Brazil Squadron). Back in American waters in mid-1861, he took command of the *Cambridge* in the Atlantic Blockading Squadron. In the fall and early winter, Cushing was among his junior officers. Gwin was transferred to the Mississippi Squadron in January 1862 as captain of the timberclad gunboat *Tyler*. On the evening and through the first night of the battle of Shiloh, the *Tyler* and her sister ship, *Lexington*, provided covering fire for the reorganization of Union forces. Promoted to lieutenant commander, Gwin commanded the ironclad *Mound City* in the summer of 1862 and then took command of the navy's largest ironclad, the *Benton*. Covering Sherman's landing at Chickasaw Bluffs on the Yazoo River north of Vicksburg, on December 27, 1862, Gwin was mortally wounded. He died January 3, 1863.

Howorth, William L.

Ensign, USN. An officer aboard the *Monticello*, Howorth was one of Cushing's most dedicated followers, accompanying him on several raids, including the sinking of the *Albemarle*.

Jones, J. E.

Ensign, USN. An officer aboard the *Monticello*. One of Cushing's volunteers on several raids.

Jones, Thomas Marshall

Colonel, CSA. USMA 1853. Born: Virginia. Resigning his commission as a first lieutenant in 1861, Jones joined the Confederate army as colonel of the 29th Mississippi. He resigned that position after the battle of Stones River (Murfreesboro) December 31, 1862–January 2, 1863. He was in command of Fort Caswell on the North Carolina coast at the time of Cushing's raid in late February 1864.

Lamson, Roswell H.

Lieutenant, USN. USNA 1862. 1837–1903. Born: Iowa. Lamson commanded the USS *Mount Vernon* in the rivers and sounds of North Carolina, often cooperating with his colleagues Flusser and Cushing. Later he commanded the converted blockade-runner *Gettysburg*. He piloted the powder ship *Louisiana* in the attempt to blow up Fort Fisher on December 23, 1864, during Butler's failed attempt on the fort. He resigned from the navy in 1866. He died in Oregon. His journal, *Lamson of the Gettysburg*, is one of the best accounts of the Civil War navy.

Lay, John L.

The engineer Cushing credited with inventing the spar torpedo he used to sink the *Albemarle*.

Lee, Robert E.

General, CSA. 1807–1870. USMA: 1829 (2/46). Born: Virginia. The preeminent general of the Confederacy, Lee distinguished himself from West Point onward. He was a member of the Corps of Engineers, a hero of the Mexican War, superintendent of West Point, and second in command of the elite Second Cavalry. On leave in the capital at the time of John Brown's raid on Harper's Ferry, he was dispatched with a force of marines to capture Brown and his men. Offered command of the Federal armies at the outbreak of war, he refused, resigning to defend his native state. His war service had a disappointing start with a failed campaign in western Virginia. He then commanded forces on the South Atlantic coast before being summoned to Richmond to serve as military advisor to President Jefferson Davis. On June 1, 1862, Lee replaced General Joseph E. Johnston, wounded at the battle of Seven Pines, as commander of the Confederate field army that would shortly after become the Army of Northern Virginia. Over the next three years, Lee and his army established a record rarely equaled in military history. Lee became commander of all the Confederate armies in February 1865 when the Southern cause was already doomed. He surrendered to Lieutenant General Ulysses S. Grant on April 9, 1865. Postwar he became president of Washington University, which became Washington and Lee University following his death. Although some recent biographers have attempted to reduce Lee's reputation as a general and as a man, he remains the most revered of Civil War figures after Abraham Lincoln.

Lee, Samuel Phillips

Rear Admiral, USN. 1812–1897. Born: Fairfax County, Virginia. The grandson of the Revolutionary hero Richard Henry Lee and a cousin of

Robert E. Lee, he was appointed a midshipman in 1825. He had a distinguished antebellum career, including combat in the Mexican War. A senior commander at the beginning of the Civil War, he participated in the blockade, the capture of New Orleans, and Farragut's early attempts to open the Mississippi. Promoted to acting rear admiral, he commanded the North Atlantic Blockading Squadron from September 1862 to October 1864. He was criticized for failing to close Wilmington by blockade, although he repeatedly begged for troops to attack Fort Fisher, which protected the approaches to the city. He was replaced by Rear Admiral David Dixon Porter for the combined army-navy operation that would capture the fort and close Wilmington in January 1865. Lee commanded the Mississippi Squadron for the remainder of the war. He retired in 1873. Lee was an in-law of the influential Blair family of Missouri. In *Lamson of the Gettysburg*, editors James and Patricia McPherson speculate that Lee may have been removed from command of the North Atlantic Blockading Squadron because of his connection with the Blairs. That seems unlikely. By the fall of 1864 it appeared that Lincoln would be reelected. Radical Republicans, who had been backing the candidacy of John C. Frémont since the spring, hinted that Frémont would withdraw if Lincoln fired Postmaster General Montgomery Blair, a moderate on the reconstruction of the South and the compensation of slave owners. Blair had offered to resign for the president's political convenience shortly after Lincoln was renominated in June. On September 23, a day after Frémont's withdrawal, Lincoln asked Blair for his resignation. The Blair family reacted with equanimity, continuing to back Lincoln's reelection. In his diary, Secretary of the Navy Welles recorded both surprise and chagrin at Blair's resignation. Since he had signed Lee's transfer orders a week before, it seems impossible that there was any connection with either Frémont's withdrawal or Blair's resignation. Nor does it seem likely that Lee's wife, Montgomery's strong-willed sister Elizabeth, would have accepted the family's continued support of Lincoln if her husband had been sacrificed as part of a deal to conciliate the Radical Republicans. Finally, if the administration's intent had been to sacrifice Lee for political expediency, it seems unlikely that Welles would have ordered him to another prestigious command. If Welles's diary is to be believed, and it is generally considered one of the most reliable documents of its kind, Welles's concern was not politics but Lee's tendencies toward caution and delay. The operation against Fort Fisher would require an aggressive commander with experience in joint operations with the army. After Farragut begged off for health reasons, Welles appointed Porter, who had worked closely with Grant in the capture of Vicksburg. According to Welles's diary entry on September 15: "[Assistant Secretary of the Navy] Fox tells me that Grant, with whom he has conversed, would not be satisfied with Lee. . . . It pains me to distress [Lee] and the Blairs by detaching him and ordering another to the work, but individual feeling, partialities, and friendships must not be in the way of the public welfare. . . . Admiral Porter is probably the best man for the service."

Longstreet, James

Lieutenant General, CSA. USMA 1842 (54/62). 1821–1904. Born: South Carolina. Longstreet served on the frontier and with distinction in the Mexican War. One of the Civil War's outstanding combat generals, Longstreet commanded one wing of Lee's army prior to Thomas J. (Stonewall) Jackson's death and then the largest of the three corps in the reorganized Army of Northern Virginia. The "perfect corps commander," he showed little aptitude for independent command when assigned the Department of North Carolina and Southern Virginia in the late winter and spring of 1863. At Gettysburg, his excessive deliberation and lack of enthusiasm for a fight he considered unwise contributed to Confederate defeat. Ordered to northwest Georgia to reinforce Bragg, Longstreet had his greatest day when his attack on September 20, 1863, shattered the Union right at Chickamauga and caused the rout of the Army of the Cumberland. However, the failure of his Knoxville campaign again demonstrated his lack of talent for independent command. Returning to the East, he was seriously wounded by friendly fire during the Battle of the Wilderness on May 6, 1864. Returning to duty in October, he fought through the remaining battles of the war, surrendering with Lee at Appomattox on April 9, 1865. After the war, Longstreet settled in New Orleans where he outraged die-hard Confederates by becoming a Republican during the presidency of his old friend Ulysses S. Grant. Defenders of Lee heaped blame on him for Gettysburg. The criticism of Longstreet's performance and character continues to this day among true believers in the Lost Cause.

Lynch

Master's Mate on the *Commodore Perry* under Flusser's command. Braving heavy fire, Lynch and several sailors helped Cushing wheel a howitzer into position to repel a boarding attempt from the shore of the Blackwater River on October 3, 1862. Lynch was killed in the fighting.

Lynch, William Francis

Admiral, CSA. 1801–1865. Born: Norfolk, Virginia. Entering the navy as a midshipman in 1819, Lynch enjoyed an illustrious antebellum career, serving aboard numerous sailing ships and steamers and commanding several. He led an exploring expedition to the Middle East, writing *Narrative of the United States' Expedition to the River Jordan and the Dead Sea* (Philadelphia: Lea and Blanchard, 1849). Lynch resigned his commission on April 21, 1861. Except for a brief period, he commanded Confederate naval forces in the waters of Virginia and North Carolina throughout the war. Aging and allegedly addicted to opium, he was criticized by subordinates and civilian observers for timidity and inefficiency. In the defense of Roanoke Island and Elizabeth City on February 10, 1862, Lynch directed a shore battery while his "mosquito fleet" of small gunboats was annihilated by Union gunboats in fifteen minutes. His failure to command from shipboard was denounced by many as "cowardice." He approved the building of several ironclads but failed to provide leadership in design or construction. Only the *Albemarle* saw effective service. Lynch was paroled at Richmond on May 3, 1865. He died in Baltimore the following October.

Macomb, William H.

Commander, USN. 1819–1872. Born: Michigan. Macomb saw action on the Mississippi before taking command of the USS *Shamrock*, flagship of the North Atlantic Blockading Squadron. Admiral S. P. Lee sent Macomb to recapture Plymouth after Cushing sank the *Albemarle*. In his narrative, Cushing misspelled Macomb's name as McComb.

Martin

An officer on the *Monticello*, Martin was another of the willing volunteers on some of Cushing's raids.

Mercer, Samuel

Captain, USN. 1799–1862. Mercer joined the navy as a midshipman in 1815. He served in the Mexican War as captain of the brig USS *Lawrence*. At the beginning of the Civil War, he was in command of the side-wheel frigate *Powhatan*. He led a squadron to relieve Fort Sumter but arrived too late. Succeeded in command by David Dixon Porter, Mercer took command of the newly recommissioned frigate *Wabash*, considered by many the navy's premier ship. Shortly after participating in the capture of the Cape Hatteras forts, Mercer was relieved because of age. He served on the Navy Retiring Board until his death in March 1862.

Parker, William Albert

Commander USN. 1816–? Born: Portsmouth, New Hampshire. Parker joined the navy as a midshipman in 1832, serving on many ships and stations.

He served on the frigate *Raritan* during the Mexican War and subsequently at the Naval Observatory, one of the navy's most prestigious shore assignments. He was promoted to commander and given command of the converted steamer USS *Cambridge* early in the Civil War. He subsequently commanded the James River Squadron. He retired in 1879 as a captain. He was a steady but cautious commander whom Cushing found lacking in audacity.

Peck, John James

Major General, USA(V). 1821–1878. USMA 1843 (8/39). Peck served on the frontier and won two brevets in the Mexican War. He resigned in 1853 to enter business in upstate New York, where he was active in Democratic politics. Appointed a brigadier general in August 1861, he served in brigade and division command in the Peninsular campaign. Promoted to major general, he commanded all Union forces in Virginia south of the James River. In the spring of 1863, he successfully defended Suffolk against a siege by Confederate forces under Lieutenant General James Longstreet. Although Longstreet foraged at will in the surrounding countryside during the siege, Peck's stubborn defense delayed the return of Longstreet's corps to Lee's army in time for the battle of Chancellorsville. Writing to Admiral Lee, Cushing was critical of Peck's lack of aggressiveness and overdependence on the frail gunboats patrolling the Nansemond River. Peck was seriously injured in an accident in the early summer of 1863 but returned to duty to command the District of North Carolina from August 1863 through the following April. Thereafter he commanded the Canadian frontier until mustered out in August 1865. After the war he organized the New York State Life Insurance Company, serving as its president until his death.

Porter, Benjamin H.

Lieutenant, USN. USNA 1862. c. 1845–1865. Born: New York. A friend of Cushing's from the Naval Academy, Porter had seen much active service, including capture and imprisonment in an 1863 raid on Fort Sumter. He relieved Cushing as commander of the flagship *Malvern* when Cushing returned to his old ship, the *Monticello*. Porter was killed leading his men during the naval land assault on Fort Fisher January 15, 1865. Cushing was nearby, as was Porter's best friend, Lieutenant Samuel Preston, who was also killed in the assault. Lieutenant Porter was not a relative of Admiral David D. Porter.

Porter, David Dixon

Rear Admiral, USN. 1813–1891. Born: Pennsylvania. One of the most colorful and controversial figures of the Civil War, David Dixon Porter came from an influential naval family. He was a son of Commodore David

Porter, foster brother of Admiral David Farragut, and the younger brother of Commodore William "Dirty Bill" Porter. He first went to sea at eleven, accompanying his father on an expedition against pirates in the West Indies. At thirteen he became a midshipman in the Mexican navy, having a number of adventures including incarceration in a Cuban prison. He was repatriated and appointed a midshipman in the United States Navy in 1829. He had a varied but not particularly exceptional career in the antebellum navy, his most important service coming in the Mexican War. Only a lieutenant at the beginning of the Civil War, he rose rapidly. His enemies denounced him as mendacious and ruthlessly ambitious, but Porter was also brave, energetic, innovative, and hugely competent. And, like his friend Grant, he fought while others dithered. He helped design the expedition against New Orleans, recommending Farragut for command. Farragut, in turn, named Porter commander of the fleet's mortar squadron. Although the mortars proved only marginally effective in the bombardment of Forts Jackson and St. Phillip, Porter forced the surrender of the garrisons once Farragut had run his ships past. Not blind to his failings, Secretary of the Navy Gideon Welles and Assistant Secretary Gustavus Fox recognized Porter's ability and boldness. At their urging, Lincoln elevated Porter to acting rear admiral and gave him command of the Mississippi River Squadron after a wound incapacitated Commodore Andrew Foote. Porter found Grant and Sherman commanders much to his liking, and together they waged the decisive campaign to open the Mississippi that climaxed with the capture of Vicksburg on July 4, 1863. The Red River campaign in the spring of 1864 failed as utterly as the Vicksburg campaign had succeeded brilliantly, Porter barely extricating his fleet. In October 1864, he took command of the North Atlantic Blockading Squadron with the primary mission of capturing Fort Fisher and closing the Confederacy's last major port at Wilmington, North Carolina. Porter and Major General Alfred Terry accomplished this in January 1865. After the war Porter was superintendent of the Naval Academy. In 1870 he succeeded Farragut as admiral of the navy. In retirement he wrote his memoirs and several novels.

Preston, Samuel W.

Flag Lieutenant, USN. USNA 1861. c. 1845–1865. A friend of Cushing's from the Naval Academy, Preston had been captured with his best friend, Benjamin Porter, in a raid on Fort Sumter in 1863. He was second in command of the powder boat *Louisiana*. He and Porter died moments apart in the naval land assault on Fort Fisher January 15, 1865.

Rhind, Alexander C.

Commander, USN. 1821–1897. Appointed a midshipman in 1838, Rhind rose steadily in the antebellum navy. At the beginning of the Civil War, he was given command of the *Crusader* in the North Atlantic Blockading Squadron. He earned a vote of thanks from Congress for destroying Confederate works on the South Edisto, Pon-Pon, and Dawho rivers in April 1862. In April 1863, he commanded the ironclad *Keokuk* in Du Pont's failed attempt to reduce the Charleston forts with a naval attack. Hit heavily and sinking, the *Keokuk* remained afloat thanks to Rhind's efforts until the crew could be taken off. Rhind captained the famous "Powder Boat" attack on Fort Fisher on December 24, 1864. The USS *Louisiana*, a 143-foot-long iron-hulled steamer, was loaded with 430,000 pounds of powder—an immense floating bomb whose explosion was intended to bury Fort Fisher's guns and kill or incapacitate the garrison. The brainchild of Major General Benjamin Butler, the "Powder Boat" was a spectacular failure. The navy's munitions experts failed to properly fuse the explosive, and Rhind failed to ground the vessel close to the fort before abandoning ship. The ship floated a half-mile offshore, the fuses failed, and the fire left behind by Rhind ignited only part of the powder. Many in the fort's garrison slept through the explosion. In his memoir, Cushing called the failure none of Rhind's fault, but elsewhere he was critical of the failure to get the *Louisiana* closer to the fort. Rhind continued in the navy after the war, eventually becoming a rear admiral.

Sands, Benjamin F.

Captain, USN. 1812–1883. Born: Baltimore, Maryland. Appointed a midshipman in 1828, he saw extensive antebellum service, including service in the Mexican War and command of the steamer *Walker*. A specialist in coastal surveying, he continued in this capacity until 1863, when he was ordered to duty with the North Atlantic Blockading Squadron as commander of the steam sloop *Dacotah*. Because of his seniority, he was frequently the senior officer on the scene in areas within the extensive blockade. Cushing ran afoul of Sands when the latter refused to detail men for a raid up the Cape Fear River to destroy the ironclad *Raleigh* in May–June 1864 until ordered to do so by Admiral S. D. Lee, to whom Cushing had also presented his plan. Sands commanded the large side-wheel steamer *Fort Jackson* in operations against Fort Fisher at the turn of the year 1864–1865. In 1867, Sands was made superintendent of the Naval Observatory at Washington, developing the observatory to rank among the best in the world. He was promoted to rear admiral in 1871. He retired in 1874.

Shuttleworth, William Louis

Major, USMC. 1812–1871. Born: Piscataway, New Jersey. Shuttleworth served as a carpenter in the navy 1831–1839, when he resigned and joined the marine corps as a second lieutenant. He was brevetted captain for gallantry in the marine assault on Vera Cruz in the Mexican War but was not promoted to the substantive rank until 1857. He led the fleet's marines in the assault on Forts Hatteras and Clark on August 28, 1861, during which time Cushing referred to him as "old Major Shuttleworth," although it does not appear from the record that he was promoted to major until 1864, but it is quite possible he had been promoted by brevet. After two years aboard the *Minnesota*, Shuttleworth took command of the marine detachment at the Pensacola Navy Yard. In 1864 he was promoted through the substantive grades of major and lieutenant colonel to colonel. He retired in 1869.

Smith, Joseph B.

Lieutenant, USN. USNA 1847. 1826–1862. Born: Belfast, Maine. Smith had a successful if uneventful antebellum career. In 1860, he was appointed executive officer of the aging sail frigate *Congress*. At anchor in Hampton Roads, Smith was in acting command when the CSS *Virginia* (popularly known as the *Merrimack*) attacked. Smith was killed in the battle. Smith was the son of Commodore Joseph Smith, a cousin of Cushing's mother.

Stringham, Silas Horton

Commodore, USN. 1798–1876. Born: New York. Entering the navy as a midshipman at the age of eleven in 1809, he fought in the War of 1812 and the Mexican War, in the interim serving in the West Indies and the Mediterranean. Named commander of the Atlantic Blockading Squadron, he joined with Major General Benjamin Butler in the successful expedition that wrested control of Hatteras Inlet from the Confederacy in August 1861. Although the expedition revealed the inexperience and manifold shortcomings of Federal forces in combined and amphibious operations, Stringham's innovative deployment of the bombarding fleet guaranteed Federal success at almost no loss. Recognizing the increasing infirmities of age, Stringham requested relief from sea duty in December 1861. Promoted to rear admiral, he commanded the Boston Navy Yard for the remainder of the war.

Sumner, Edwin Vose

Major General, USA(V). 1797–1863. Born: Massachusetts. Entering the army as a second lieutenant in 1819, Sumner fought in the Blackhawk War, the Mexican War, and on the frontier. He was in command of the Department of the Pacific at the outbreak of the Civil War. He commanded II Corps of the Army of the Potomac on the Peninsula, at South Mountain, and again at Antietam under McClellan. At Fredericksburg, he commanded the Right Grand Division under Burnside. He was relieved at his own request after the battle. He died en route to a new post in Missouri. A soldier of the old school, he possessed undoubted courage and loyalty but lacked the intelligence and flexibility necessary for success in high command.

Swan, Frank
Assistant Paymaster, USN. One of Cushing's boat crew during the sinking of the *Albemarle*.

Terry, Alfred H.
Major General, USA(V). 1827–1890. Born: Hartford, Connecticut. A lawyer and militia officer before the war, Terry rose to brigadier general of volunteers on competent if unspectacular performance in a number of minor operations in the first three years of the war. Following Butler's failure against Fort Fisher in December 1864, Terry was elevated to command of the army forces in a renewal of the attack in January 1865. He cooperated fully with Admiral Porter during the landing and the subsequent two-day assault on the Confederacy's strongest fort. Its fall effectively closed Wilmington, the last major port open to blockade-runners. A delighted Congress awarded Terry a commission as a brigadier general in the Regular Army. He stayed in the army following the war, becoming a major figure in the Indian wars. Although a steady commander, Terry's appointment as a Regular Army brigadier general remains curious when perhaps a dozen other volunteer generals had combat records at least as illustrious.

Upshur, John
Lieutenant Commander USN. Captain of the *Advance*. (In his memoir, Cushing referred to the *Advance* as the *A. D. Vance*, the name under which the steamer had operated as a blockade-runner before its capture on September 10, 1864, by Union blockaders.) Cushing bitterly criticized Upshur for claiming a share of the prize money for the capture of the *Charlotte* and *Stag*. Although Cushing could be harshly critical of other officers' performance, he does not appear to have had many personal enemies, making his enmity toward Upshur stand out.

Valentine, Edward K.
Masters Mate, USN. Serving aboard the USS *Ellis*, Valentine was one of Cushing's most devoted followers on several of his early raids.

Welles, Gideon

Secretary of the United States Navy. 1802–1878. Born: Connecticut. A newspaper editor, politician, and former employee of the Navy Department, Welles was named secretary of the Navy by Lincoln in 1861. He proved an inspired choice, supervising the expansion of the navy from 90 to 670 ships and from 9,000 to 57,000 men. Welles and Assistant Secretary Gustavus Fox, a navy captain, worked together superbly, Fox handling the administration of the fleet while Welles fought the department's political battles. As unflappable as Secretary of War Stanton was mercurial, Welles was a steadying influence on the cabinet. He resigned in 1869 to return to journalism. His three-volume *Diary* (1911) is a major source for students of naval affairs in the Civil War.

Wessels, Henry W.

Brigadier General, USA(V). USMA 1833 (29/43). 1809–1889. Born: Connecticut. Wessels saw service on the frontier and in the Mexican War, rising to the rank of major. In the Civil War, he served on the Peninsula and in North Carolina. Competent but never inspired, he defended Plymouth, North Carolina, until forced to surrender on April 20, 1864, the day after the *Albemarle*'s victory over Flusser's squadron. Exchanged, he did not return to field duty. He continued in the Regular Army after the war, retiring in 1871.

Wood, W. W.

Chief Engineer, USN. Prepared the spar torpedo that Cushing used to sink the *Albemarle*.

Woodman, John

Acting Masters Mate, USN. A member of the raid on the *Albemarle*, Woodman drowned despite Cushing's attempt to tow him to shore.

Worden, John L.

Captain, USN. 1818–1897. Born: New York. Entering the navy as a midshipman in 1835, he served at sea and at the Naval Observatory. Captured early in the war while delivering orders to Fort Pickens, Florida, he was a prisoner until October 1861. He assisted John Ericsson in the construction of the *Monitor* and took it into battle against the *Virginia/Merrimack* on March 9, 1862, where he was seriously wounded. Promoted to commander and then captain, he commanded the ironclad *Montauk* in the South Atlantic Blockading Squadron until June 1863. He spent the remainder of the war supervising the construction of ironclads. He retired as a rear admiral in 1886.

Index

༄

About the Editor

Alden R. Carter is a former naval officer and teacher. He has published more than forty books for children, young adults, and adults. His novels for young people have won numerous honors, including six American Library Association Best Book awards. His adult novel *Bright Starry Banner* was named the Best Civil War Novel of 2004 by the Military Order of the Stars and Bars. Mr. Carter has made more than 500 presentations on writing. Named to the Wisconsin Library Association's list of "Notable Wisconsin Authors" in 2002, he lives in Marshfield, Wisconsin, with his wife, the fabric artist and photographer Carol Shadis Carter. They have two adult children, Brian and Siri.